Dinner at Our Place

Dinner at Our Place

Recipes for Gathering

SHIZA SHAHID
AND FRIENDS OF
Our Place

HARVEST
An Imprint of WILLIAM MORROW

To those who taught us to cook, eat, and gather. Thanks for making this place ours.

CONTENTS

This is a book about gathering.

The importance of it, the joyful act of it, and—of course—the people around the table. It's a truism that food brings people together. Its power to connect has stood the tests of time, stressful holidays, and the scrutiny of in-laws all over the world. Despite the odds (or because we're hungry), we are always coming back to the table for more.

Consider this your solution to a specific problem: It can be hard to get together over a home-cooked meal. Schedules are chaotic. It feels like a big To Do. You've always wanted to host a proper dinner party, but you never knew where to start. Lighting a wheel of cheese on fire sounds totally cool, but . . . *how*? This book is here to put to rest the notion that you have to be some sort of expert to cook and host. You don't. Like so much else in this life, it's a skill that you can pick up and learn. Lucky for you, it's pretty intuitive at the end of the day. Gathering with the people you love and eating yummy foods *should* be exciting and easy, after all. But we understand the parts of hosting that trip us up, stress us out, and make us hesitate before sending out the invitations. *Dinner at Our Place* was born to banish those fears and empower you to host, in whatever way works for you. It's here to plan and plot with you and for you. To inspire new ways of being and eating with whomever you call your people. To take the mental load off of you, the host, by doing all of that work for you. To create new traditions and strengthen old ones.

This is not your typical cookbook.

In an ideal world, we'd be throwing dinner parties at least once a month. This book exists in that ideal world. In fact, the whole point of this book is to transform that ideal world into a reality. Here's the gist: Within these pages lies everything you need to cook and host spectacular dinner parties. Okay, not *everything*. This is not a magical object that can do your grocery shopping, but it will make writing out your list deceptively easy. From full menu plans to detailed recipes, conversation starters, tablescapes, florals, playlists, and beyond, *Dinner at Our Place* is here to make throwing a dinner party achievable—and joyful. It's a comprehensive playbook for hosting. It *is* your excuse to throw a party together. It's an accessible

SO YOU WANT TO THROW A DINNER PARTY?

DO YOU HAVE A TABLE?

Yes

No

Groovy.

All good. Dinner parties are defined by people and food, not furniture.

DO YOU LIKE TO COOK?

Yes

No

Make cooking a party and you might change your mind.

DO YOUR FRIENDS LIKE TO EAT?

Yes

There is only one answer.

Conclusion: You're ready to host dinner parties.

guide for cooking seasonally and making the most of what's around you. It's made for those of us interested in cooking, gathering, and sharing our cultures, and it's bound to provide a few firsts to hosts, seasoned and unseasoned alike.

This book is by and for home cooks.

You might be wondering what these dinner parties entail and who created them. Each chapter—of which there are twelve, or a year's worth of monthly dinner parties—was lovingly shared by a home cook whose reputation as host, curator, gathering specialist precedes them. While many of these home cooks are chefs, culinary directors, food stylists, or cookbook authors in their own right, what's in these pages here is of a more personal nature. These are the recipes they're known for making for their families, given or chosen. And you're invited to take part in their celebrations, to pull up a chair of your own, and enjoy some of the best, most tried and true, dinner parties we've ever encountered.

Let's say it's December and you're hosting your very first hot pot night. Lucky for you, Keegan and Mama Fong, the mother-son duo behind Woon in Los Angeles, have shared in *precise* detail how to pull this off. Considering they've been hosting some version of this party since Keegan was in high school,

when teenagers would crowd the house demanding hot pot by shouting da bin lo, we trust them. Whether it's hot pot or making a summer Caribbean feast with DeVonn Francis or trying your hand at Jen Monroe's genius, meltable butter candles for bread dipping, the following pages are rich with cooking tips and traditions that have been honed and perfected by some of the coolest tastemakers we know. Borrow freely from their experiences. Learn clever substitutions, how to navigate a farmers' market, what kinds of things to pick up on your travels, how to delegate in the kitchen. These dinner parties are not only delicious, but they're fun—and they're the sum of decades of cooking and hosting experience. And it's all written down and yours for the taking.

This book is for building traditions.

We believe that the best connections are made across the kitchen table. There's possibly no greater joy than getting together with your people, eating something your hands made, and lingering around the table swapping stories, catching up, and getting to know one another more, better. Something special happens when you cook for others. It's the care you take with each step in the recipe or with each plate passed around the table. It's the ritualistic reverence with which you prepare your home for guests. It's the

generosity of the home cooks who made this book will inspire something in you, too. Maybe it'll inspire you to simply open up your home or offer to cook in someone else's. Maybe it'll be that thing that forges a new friendship. Maybe it will inspire a dinner party book club among your friend group. Maybe it'll be the beginning of a tradition you carry on for years and years and years. We can only hope that the recipes and essays laid before you can have so much power. Because if there's anything we believe in, it's the power of home cooking to bring people together.

excitement you're filled with as the clock approaches seven or the guessing game you make out of who is going to arrive first (and who will be last). It is its own kind of tradition, one we're very keen on building.

Traditions of every make and variety have felt increasingly hard to keep and even harder to make anew. We want traditions that reflect who we are, where we came from, and where we're going, but it can be a challenge—especially as a young person—to establish that for oneself and one's community. Our larger looming hope for *Dinner at Our Place* is that it will help you establish new, longstanding traditions, and that it will serve as a blueprint for making those traditions distinctly yours. We hope that the collective

WHAT'S INCLUDED
Recipes
Menus
Vibes
Conversations
Bar Setups
Tablescapes
Playlists

YOU
Position yourself in the best seat to
slip in and out of the room.

YOUR SHY FRIEND
Sit them next to you so
that you can encourage
them in conversation.

YOUR CHATTY FRIEND
Always the reliable
storyteller, this friend
can sit anywhere and
be the glue for the
dinner party.

Social Dynamics
Perfectly Balanced

YOUR CRUSH
Sit them close enough
that you can converse,
but far enough away that
you have to ask them to
pass the salt.

YOUR NEW FRIEND
Put them next to your
bestie since they'll
inevitably be friends
with them, too.

YOUR BESTIE
Anchor them at the other end of the table,
ensuring you can make eyes at each other.

Tools to Enable Gathering

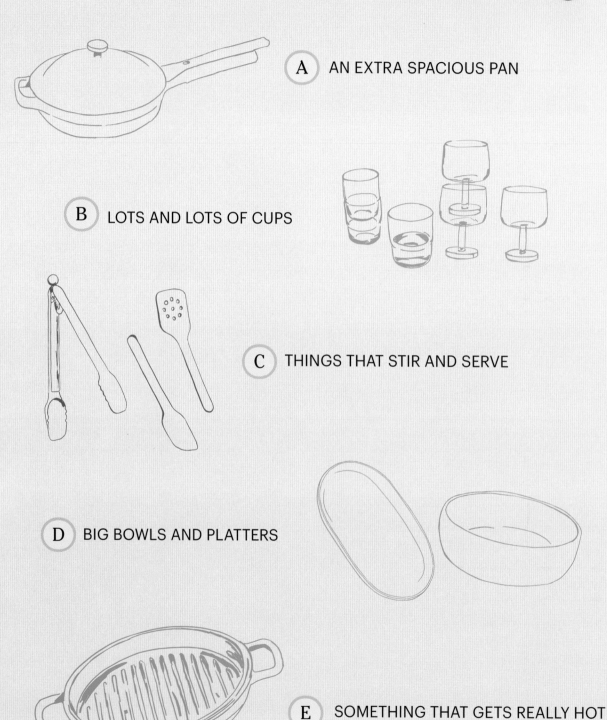

A · AN EXTRA SPACIOUS PAN

B · LOTS AND LOTS OF CUPS

C · THINGS THAT STIR AND SERVE

D · BIG BOWLS AND PLATTERS

E · SOMETHING THAT GETS REALLY HOT

My favorite
conversations are usually
about _____.

What is the best
compliment you have
ever received?

How do you
define home?

What's the craziest
thing you've ever
done for love?

How do you define
indulgence?

Tell us about the most
fun night you've had in
the last year.

Family Dinner

WITH SHIZA SHAHID

Shiza is a self-taught home cook and host extraordinaire. With over a decade of experience bringing people together, her hosting style is raw, vulnerable, and cathartic. She believes in the power of gathering so much that she cofounded Our Place to enable others to cook and eat together.

JANUARY

STEAL MY PLAYLIST

My dinner parties began as an antidote to loneliness. I was twenty-two years old in New York City, living seven thousand miles away from my home in Pakistan, and working way too much. I missed my amma's cooking. I missed the warm weather.

And I missed having a community to lean on. As any New Yorker can tell you, being lonely did not mean I was alone. I was swept up in the nonprofit world, spending many nights at galas and fundraising events—essentially multicourse "dinner parties" that had a very good way of leaving me feeling drained and disconnected. They were a far cry from my preferred way of breaking bread with people, especially conversationally. Just picture it: You're locked into a seating chart, it's shockingly noisy, and topics stay superficial all night. In a weird way, these events inspired my first dinner parties; I wanted to take a radically opposite approach to bringing people together. And so, I did.

I started hosting dinner parties on a monthly basis. My studio apartment didn't have room for a dining table, so I'd ask friends and friends of friends if I could use theirs, and people were surprisingly generous. Now I'm in Los Angeles, which is—lucky for me—more sprawling, so I have the luxury of owning a table that fits my ideal dinner party size: eight to twelve people (sixteen, if you're determined enough). This number keeps it big enough that not everyone knows each other, but small enough that everyone can *get* to know each other. In the spirit of getting everyone to feel connected, I have a few best practices. Candles and arrangements are to be kept low so everyone can see one another. While there is music, it's turned down so that even the gentlest of voices can be heard. And now, I have my signature practice: I always have a prompt. While pocket conversations and one-on-one connections are a sign of a successful dinner party, I like to be sure there's a central moment when everyone is engaged in a single conversation. Hence, the prompt. I have a stronger-than-average aversion

to small talk, so these prompts are designed to do the exact opposite, creating deep, meaningful connections from the start. They give everyone a chance to speak and be heard. They take the conversation places it wouldn't otherwise go. I've been doing this for years and years, and it has become foundational to how I host and grow my chosen family.

Speaking of family, this particular dinner party centers around my belief that family can be anyone who's at your table. In honor of that, this Family Dinner menu is a representation of my many identities and the many families I've made over the years. There are recipes full of the spices from my childhood in Pakistan. There are Persian foods to honor my partner and the family we created together. And, of course, there are some distinctly Californian dishes that celebrate the new home I have created for myself so far away from my roots. I particularly like hosting a dinner party in January because it comes on the heels of spending the winter break back in Pakistan. I pretty much start planning it the moment I get off the sixteen-hour flight, the jet lag only making things look a little less orthodox. Curating guest lists at 3 a.m., calling to confirm an ingredient with amma at 6 a.m. I could wait, of course, but I find those first days of return invigorating, as if I am in both Pakistan and California at the same time, if only for a little while.

It is both a challenge and an honor to embody multiple identities at once, and this menu is a reflection of that and my attempt to share more of myself with my community. Luckily, food can always be that for us: an extension of ourselves that we can offer up to others. A part of who we are and the cultures we belong to. And, of course, a great excuse for people to gather.

Crudités with Raita

Serves 6 to 8

One way to take the stress off of yourself while hosting is to have something plated and ready before anyone shows up. Enter: raita, a tangy, herbaceous dip that pairs beautifully with simple, raw vegetables. This highly snackable dish can be prepped in advance so all you have to do is set it out for people to enjoy.

½ cup fresh cilantro leaves

½ cup fresh mint leaves

1 English cucumber

2 cups Greek yogurt

2 teaspoons kosher salt

½ teaspoon freshly ground black pepper

1 tablespoon champagne vinegar or white wine vinegar

Grated zest and juice of 1 lemon

1 tablespoon olive oil

1 teaspoon cumin seeds, toasted and lightly crushed

Sliced seasonal vegetables, such as carrots, cucumber, endive, cherry tomatoes, etc.

1. With a pestle and mortar or small food processor, combine the cilantro and mint and smash into a paste. Set aside.

2. Using the small holes of a box grater, grate the cucumber. Place the grated cucumber into a cheesecloth or kitchen towel and squeeze, discarding the excess water.

3. Add the grated cucumber to a medium bowl. Add the herb paste, yogurt, salt, pepper, vinegar, lemon zest, olive oil, and cumin seeds. Stir well. Add a tablespoon of lemon juice (or more to taste).

4. Transfer to a dip bowl and serve alongside sliced crudités.

   Make Ahead: Prepare the raita up to a day before, storing it in an airtight container in the refrigerator.

Citrus Salad

Serves 6 to 8

California is where I learned how to cook, so it's only necessary that I honor it with my dinner party menu. And what better way to do that than with seasonal produce? Bright winter citrus takes center stage in this dish, accented by the sweet crunch of candied pecans. Make the dressing in advance and consider this another one that's easy to throw together close to dinner time. Note: If you're looking to save a little time, you can always go with store-bought candied pecans instead of candying them yourself.

Candied Pecans

¼ cup pecans

1 tablespoon maple syrup

½ teaspoon kosher salt

Mint Vinaigrette

1 tablespoon Dijon mustard

Juice of 2 lemons (about 5 to 6 tablespoons)

2 teaspoons maple syrup

2 teaspoons kosher salt, plus more to taste

1 teaspoon freshly ground black pepper, plus more to taste

¼ cup olive oil

2 tablespoons coarsely chopped fresh mint

Assembly

5.5 ounces baby spinach

2 Cara Cara oranges, peeled and thinly sliced into rounds

2 blood oranges, peeled and thinly sliced into rounds

2 navel oranges, peeled and thinly sliced into rounds

2 avocados, thinly sliced

Mint leaves, for garnish

1. Make the candied pecans: Preheat the oven to 375°F.

2. In a medium bowl, toss together the pecans, maple syrup, and salt. Spread onto a sheet pan and roast until the nuts are roasted all the way through and caramelized, about 15 minutes.

3. Remove from the oven and allow them to cool completely. Chop coarsely.

4. Make the mint vinaigrette: In a medium bowl, whisk together the mustard, lemon juice, maple syrup, salt, and pepper. Slowly stream in the olive oil, whisking constantly, until you have a loose emulsion. Stir in the mint, taste, adjust the salt and pepper, and set the bowl aside.

5. Assemble the salad: In a medium bowl, combine the spinach and 2 tablespoons of the dressing, tossing lightly. Spread the greens onto a large platter and top with the citrus and avocados. Spoon the remaining dressing on top and garnish with the candied pecans and mint.

Make Ahead: You can prepare the mint vinaigrette up to a day ahead and store it in an airtight container in the refrigerator.

Chana Masala

Serves 4 to 6

In Pakistan, chana masala wouldn't be the first dish to come to mind when you're going to host. It's home food, a simple chickpea curry. Cozy. Something my amma would make me when I was sick. And maybe it's for that very reason that I love including it in this dinner party. Rich in healing spices like ginger and turmeric, it's a dish I consider perfect for January. Another reason I love this dish is that it is gloriously hands-off. Once you temper the spices and prepare your base, you leave everything to stew, letting time aid the flavor. Ultimately, the chickpeas should reach a thick, gravy-like consistency.

¼ cup ghee

1 small yellow onion, finely chopped

1½ teaspoons cumin seeds

1 tablespoon grated fresh ginger

2 garlic cloves, finely chopped

2 teaspoons ground coriander

1 teaspoon ground cumin

1½ teaspoons ground turmeric

1½ teaspoons Kashmiri chile powder (aka lal mirch)

2½ teaspoons kosher salt

1½ cups finely chopped plum tomatoes or one 14.5-ounce can diced tomatoes

Two 15-ounce cans chickpeas, drained and rinsed

For Serving

½ bunch of cilantro, leaves picked and coarsely chopped

1 teaspoon garam masala

Finely chopped yellow onion (optional)

1-inch piece fresh ginger, peeled and julienned (optional)

1 lemon, cut into wedges, for squeezing

1. In a medium pan, heat the ghee over medium heat until hot and shimmering. Add the onion and cook until soft and light golden brown, about 10 minutes.

2. Add the cumin seeds and toast until fragrant, about 2 minutes. Add the ginger and garlic and cook until fragrant and barely starting to get color, about 4 minutes.

3. Add the coriander, cumin, turmeric, chile powder, and salt and cook, stirring often, until the spices have bloomed lightly and the mixture has darkened in color, about 2 minutes.

4. Add the tomatoes and stir often until they start to break down, 7 to 10 minutes. Add the chickpeas and 2 cups water, stirring well to combine everything.

5. Bring the chana masala to a boil. Reduce the heat to maintain a soft simmer and cook until you have a gravy that coats the chickpeas and the back of a spoon, about 25 minutes.

6. Use your spoon to lightly smash two-thirds of the chickpeas, adding ½ cup water if the masala gets too thick. Taste for salt and adjust accordingly.

7. Garnish with the cilantro, garam masala, some chopped onion (if using), and the julienned ginger (if using). Serve with the lemon wedges.

Tandoori Chicken

Serves 6 to 8

The so-called karahi cut might as well have been invented for dinner parties. It yields smaller, more shareable cuts that make it easier to not overload your plate with one protein. Back home, we'd regularly ask the butcher for a karahi cut of chicken, which is for 16 smaller pieces versus the traditional 8. Your butcher should be able to cut your chicken this way, but you can also cleaver the pieces further at home if you're up for it. The key to this recipe is encouraging as much flavor as possible. Good news! You already did that with the karahi cut, which creates more surface area for seasoning and gives you more access to the bone. Step number two is letting the chicken marinate up to 48 hours in advance. The next comes at the very end of cooking when you high-broil the chicken until the skin is peak crispy. Of course, feel free to adjust the spice levels up or down to your liking.

3 pounds bone-in, skin-on chicken parts (drumsticks, thighs, breasts)

1 cup Greek yogurt

2 garlic cloves, finely chopped

1 tablespoon grated fresh ginger

1 tablespoon kosher salt

2 teaspoons freshly ground black pepper

1 tablespoon ground turmeric

2 teaspoons Kashmiri chile powder

2 teaspoons ground cumin

1 teaspoon anise seeds, ground

1 small pod black cardamom, ground

½ teaspoon ground cinnamon

2 lemons, 1 juiced, 1 cut into wedges

¼ cup ghee, melted

½ bunch of cilantro, leaves picked and coarsely chopped

1. In a large bowl, combine the chicken, yogurt, garlic, ginger, salt, black pepper, turmeric, Kashmiri chile powder, cumin, anise seeds, cardamom, cinnamon, and lemon juice. Toss to coat the chicken well. Cover or transfer to an airtight container and marinate in the fridge for 24 to 48 hours.

2. An hour before cooking, remove the chicken from the refrigerator and leave on the counter to take the chill off.

3. Preheat the oven to 400°F. Coat a half-sheet pan with the melted ghee.

4. Spread the chicken in an even layer on the pan and transfer to the oven. Cook until the chicken starts to form a crust, the juices are running clear, and the internal temperature is between 150° and 155°F, 20 to 25 minutes, rotating the pan and turning the chicken over halfway through.

5. Turn the broiler on high and continue cooking until the skin edges start to char and the chicken is a crusty brown, anywhere from 2 to 5 minutes depending on your broiler. Make sure the internal temperature does not exceed 160°F, as the chicken will continue cooking as it rests.

6. Remove from the oven and allow the chicken to rest before transferring it to a platter along with all the juices. Sprinkle with the cilantro and serve with the lemon wedges for squeezing.

Quick-Pickled Carrot Salad with Yogurt & Dukkah

Serves 6 to 8

This recipe includes . . . another recipe: dukkah, a wonderful, crunchy topping I grew up with that you'll love on all sorts of dishes. You can easily multiply the quantities listed below and store this as a pantry staple. Feel free to add fennel and cumin seeds to your pantry stock. I left those seeds out of the dukkah here because they were already in the salad dressing, but they'll make your pantry dukkah all the better. The carrots—which are roasted and then left to marinate in a vinaigrette—are the kind of cooked carrots I would feed someone who says they hate cooked carrots. They still pack a little bit of that desirable crunch and lend just the right level of earthiness to balance the delightful tang of the yogurt. As someone who learned to cook later in life, I am always looking for easy ways to impress my dinner guests. Spreading yogurt sauces (or any sauce, really) on the bottom of the platter rather than trying to drizzle them on top of the dish is one such hack.

Pickled Roasted Carrots

1 pound carrots, peeled and cut crosswise
  on a diagonal into 1-inch pieces
5 tablespoons olive oil
Kosher salt and freshly ground black pepper
2 tablespoons champagne vinegar,
  plus more to taste
1 tablespoon honey
1 shallot, thinly sliced
1½ teaspoons cumin seeds, toasted
1½ teaspoons fennel seeds, toasted

Dukkah

¼ cup salted roasted pistachios
2 tablespoons white sesame seeds, toasted
1 teaspoon kosher salt

Yogurt Sauce

1 cup Greek yogurt
Juice of 1 lemon
1 tablespoon honey
1 medium garlic clove, grated
Kosher salt and freshly ground black pepper

½ bunch of cilantro or mint, leaves picked and
  coarsely chopped

Make Ahead: Prepare the dukkah up to 2 weeks before, storing it in an airtight container in the refrigerator.

1. Make the pickled roasted carrots: Preheat the oven to 375°F.

2. Toss the carrots on a sheet pan with 2 tablespoons of the olive oil and salt and pepper to taste. Roast the carrots until caramelized and slightly tender, about 25 minutes.

3. Meanwhile, in a medium bowl, combine the remaining 3 tablespoons olive oil, the vinegar, honey, shallot, cumin seeds, fennel seeds, and salt and pepper to taste. Add more vinegar for acidity if needed. Set aside.

4. Make the dukkah: In a food processor, combine the pistachios, sesame seeds, and salt and process to a fine meal that can be sprinkled on top of the salad.

5. Once the carrots have roasted and then cooled slightly, transfer to the bowl with the dressing and toss to combine. Set aside to marinate for 15 to 20 minutes.

6. Make the yogurt sauce: In a medium bowl, combine the yogurt, lemon juice, honey, garlic, and salt and pepper to taste.

7. To plate, spread the yogurt sauce on the bottom of a large platter and arrange the carrots, along with any dressing from the bowl, on top. Sprinkle with the dukkah and cilantro to serve.

Saffron Tachin

Serves 8 to 10

This dish is the backbone of the dinner party menu. Like its popular cousin tahdig, tachin requires a 180-degree flip, but tachin uses more ghee and egg to make it fluffier and a touch more indulgent, which is why it's my go-to. The flip is a lot less intimidating if you use an Our Place Flipping Platter, which was designed in honor of these exact dishes.

If you are a rice-washing skeptic, please do not skip this step for this recipe! Removing the starch is key to making the tachin fluffy. Another key step is to parcook the rice 80 percent in an open boil before mixing in the rest of the ingredients and finishing it in the pan. You'll know the grains are ready when they've expanded and start floating to the top. Lastly, if you've never worked with saffron, it's okay! A little goes a long way, which is good considering the spice is worth more than its weight in gold (literally). By allowing the saffron to bloom in warm water, you're ensuring the flavor is at its most potent and evenly spread throughout the dish.

2 cups basmati rice

Kosher salt

¼ teaspoon saffron threads, lightly crushed

½ cup yogurt

2 egg yolks

3 tablespoons ghee, melted

2 tablespoons coarsely chopped fresh cilantro (optional)

2 tablespoons coarsely chopped fresh mint (optional)

3 tablespoons coarsely chopped pink pistachios (optional)

1. Rinse the basmati rice three times until the water runs clear. Then soak in a bowl for 1 hour.

2. Bring a large pot of lightly salted water to a boil. Drain the rice, add to the boiling water, and cook until parboiled, 5 to 7 minutes. Drain.

3. In the meantime, in a large bowl, combine the saffron and 2 tablespoons warm water. Set aside, allowing it to steep, about 10 minutes.

4. To the large bowl with the saffron water, add the yogurt, egg yolks, and melted ghee. Gently fold in the rice, mixing well and taking care to avoid breaking the rice.

5. Set an Always Pan over medium-low heat and add the yogurt rice, spreading with a spoon and lightly packing it down in an even layer. Using the handle of a spoon, poke 5 to 6 holes through the rice to the bottom of the pan. Cover with a lid and cook until crispy and golden brown on the bottom, 20 to 25 minutes, rotating the pan 180 degrees halfway through (at about 10 minutes) for even browning. Do not lift the lid at any point during this time. Knowing when it's ready is a bit of a guessing game since you cannot see the bottom of the pan, but you should hear a faint snap and crackle sound and smell a toasted, nutty aroma. Turn off the heat and allow the rice to steam, about 15 minutes.

6. Using a silicone or offset spatula, gently release the rice from the pan and flip it onto the Flipping Platter to serve. If desired, garnish with the cilantro, mint, and pistachios.

Crispy Potatoes with Chaat Masala

Serves 6 to 8

Crispy potatoes are a great unifier, and it's good to have at least one of those kinds of dishes at a dinner party where you're bringing all different kinds of people together. This recipe is an homage to a very specific kind of street French fry that I grew up eating as a rare treat. Admittedly, this recipe is no re-creation of the street fry. In fact, I am convinced those specific crinkle fries only exist in Pakistan. But the spirit is in this recipe nonetheless. Of course, you could always stop at "crispy potato" and no one would complain, but I like to take it a step further with homemade chaat masala (store-bought is fine, too!) to give it that extra nostalgic taste—a salty, funky, sour edge that makes the dish extra dynamic. If you're having trouble sourcing any of the spices, try your local natural foods store or look online.

Potatoes

Kosher salt

3 pounds baby potatoes

½ cup olive oil

Chaat Masala

3 tablespoons cumin seeds

1 tablespoon coriander seeds

1 teaspoon fennel seeds

1 teaspoon ajwain seeds

2 green cardamom pods

¼ cup amchur (mango) powder

2 tablespoons black salt (kala namak)

1 tablespoon kosher salt

1 teaspoon freshly ground black pepper

1 teaspoon Kashmiri chile powder

Make Ahead: Prepare the chaat masala up to 2 weeks before, storing it in an airtight container in the refrigerator.

1. Position a rack in the center of the oven and preheat the oven to 400°F.

2. Prepare the potatoes: Bring a large pot of water to a boil and season well with salt. Add the potatoes and cook until barely tender, but not falling apart, 8 to 10 minutes. Drain and allow to cool until they are safe to handle.

3. Spread the potatoes onto a sheet pan and toss in the oil, making sure all the potatoes are covered. Using the bottom of a small dish or a glass, smash the potatoes until very thin and flat.

4. Transfer to the oven and roast until the potatoes are crispy and deep golden brown, 20 to 25 minutes, tossing halfway.

5. Meanwhile, make the chaat masala: In a small pan, toast the cumin, coriander, fennel, ajwain, and cardamom over medium heat, stirring frequently, until crackling, toasty, and fragrant, about 3 minutes. Transfer the spices to a plate and allow to cool.

6. Once cooled, transfer all the spices to a spice grinder, and add the amchur powder, black salt, kosher salt, black pepper, and chile powder, and process into a fine powder.

7. Once the potatoes are roasted, transfer to a platter and dust generously with the chaat masala. Serve immediately.

Fesenjoon

Serves 6 to 8

The first time you try fesenjoon is almost always an experience. As a sweet, sour, pomegranate-forward dish, it is famously divisive and people either love it—passionately—or hate it with equal fervor. I, obviously, am in the love camp. My first time trying it was in Pakistan at my neighbor's home-slash-restaurant. (It's a very old-school Islamabad thing to open a restaurant in your home.) What this dish lacks in photogenic appeal, it more than makes up for in deliciousness. My first bite is one of my most unforgettable food memories; I had never tasted anything like it. It's sweet but earthy, robust yet simple. Made of mostly just walnuts and pomegranate molasses, it somehow, magically, becomes so much more than the sum of its parts. This recipe, which is inspired by Naz Deravian's from her book Bottom of the Pot, *is an ode to my Persian mother-in-law and, of course, her son, my partner, who—among many other things—shares my love of fesenjoon.*

If this is your first time making (or trying!) fesenjoon, I encourage you to play around with it. This recipe is a vegetarian version, but it's commonly cooked with chicken and served over rice. Consistency is also a very personal preference. You can add or subtract water to achieve your preferred thickness. You can also adjust the sweetness with a little bit of sugar. Enjoy with the Saffron Tachin (page 15).

1 pound walnuts

1 cup pomegranate molasses, plus more to taste

½ teaspoon ground turmeric

½ teaspoon kosher salt

Brown sugar (optional)

Dried pomegranate seeds, for garnish

1. In a blender or food processor, grind or pulse the walnuts until you get a fine meal. Add 2 to 3 cups of water and blend until it becomes a paste; start with the 2 cups and see how much more you need.

2. In a medium pot, combine the pomegranate molasses, turmeric, and salt. Set over medium-low heat and once it starts to bubble, stir in the walnut mixture and 1 cup water. Bring the mixture to a low simmer and cook, stirring frequently and adding more water in ½-cup increments, until slightly thickened, lightly coating the back of a spoon, and dark brown in color, at least 30 minutes. The longer you cook it, the more the flavors mix together. Taste and adjust the flavors to your liking, adding some brown sugar for added sweetness or more pomegranate molasses for tart.

3. Garnish with dried pomegranate seeds.

Zesty Cardamom Apple Crisp

Serves 8 to 10

If there is one thing that I find hard to turn down, it is a fruit-forward dessert. This recipe is my personal spin on the American classic apple cobbler. In place of butter and sugar, I opt for coconut oil and maple syrup for a sweet flavor and richness that is less on the nose (and a little healthier!). I add rose water, green cardamom, and cinnamon as an ode to the flavors I grew up with. And, for ease, I make everything in the cast-iron Always Pan and serve directly from it when the time comes. This crisp gives me the perfect I'm-walking-to-the-table-with-something-exciting *moment.*

8 Granny Smith apples, peeled and sliced ½ inch thick (6 cups)

¾ cup maple syrup

2 tablespoons fresh lemon juice

1 tablespoon vanilla extract

1 tablespoon rose water

¼ cup cornstarch

¾ teaspoon kosher salt

2 teaspoons ground cardamom

1 teaspoon ground cinnamon

2 cups almond flour

1 cup pecans, finely chopped

¾ cup coconut oil

Orange Cream

2 cups heavy cream

1 tablespoon maple syrup

Grated zest of 2 oranges

1. Preheat the oven to 375°F.

2. In a medium bowl, toss together the apples, ½ cup of the maple syrup, the lemon juice, vanilla, rose water, cornstarch, ¼ teaspoon of the salt, the cardamom, and cinnamon. Set aside.

3. In a medium bowl, gently combine the almond flour, pecans, coconut oil, remaining ¼ cup maple syrup, and remaining ½ teaspoon salt. Using your fingers or a fork, combine everything together into a shaggy shortbread.

4. To a cast-iron pan, add the apples and all the collected juices in an even layer. Using a ¼-cup measuring cup, scoop and gently press the shortbread mixture into ½-inch-thick pucks and layer on top of the fruit.

5. Transfer to the oven and bake until the apples are bubbling and the topping is golden brown, about 40 minutes.

6. In the meantime, make the orange cream: In a medium bowl, whisk together the heavy cream, maple syrup, and orange zest until stiff peaks form. Keep cold in the refrigerator until ready to serve.

7. Once the crisp is done, remove from the oven and allow to cool slightly before adding dollops of orange cream and serving.

Pear Spritz

Serves 6

I firmly believe that spritzes have just as much business showing up in the winter months as they do in the summer. Swap the bright aperitivos for sweet and earthy nectars and there you have it: a wintry spritz that's no less celebratory. Since everyone has varying preferences of sweetness levels, I recommend starting with a pear juice that has zero added sugars. You can easily increase the sweetness with a bit of maple syrup should you (or any of your guests) desire.

3 cups pear juice or pear nectar

¼ cup fresh lemon juice (from 1 to 2 lemons)

1 tablespoon orange bitters

One 750 mL bottle dry champagne

Lemon peel or sliced pear (unpeeled), for garnish

1. In a pitcher, stir together the pear juice, lemon juice, and orange bitters.

2. Fill six drinking glasses one-third of the way with the batched base, then top with champagne.

3. Garnish with lemon peel or a pear slice.

What's in a Cup (of Chai)?

Some of you may be wondering why I didn't include a recipe for chai. If you come from a culture that drinks chai, you will understand how deeply personal these recipes are. They don't just vary from region to region or household to household, but from person to person or even mood to mood. So rather than pretend that my chai is some ultimate recipe you must try (even though it is, I got it from my abba), I decided to help you discover chai your way. In order to do so, you need to understand the basic tenets of chai and experiment from there.

ELEMENTS

While chai is hyperpersonal with almost every stage and ingredient open to debate and interpretation, I will make the argument that there are a couple of boxes you need to tick for your drink to be called a cup of chai. First, you must include tea—preferably black tea and preferably loose leaf. You must also include *some kind* of milk. Preferably cow . . . and whole. (But again, I'm not here to get too prescriptive; other milks and milk alternatives are allowed.) There's a case to be made for stopping here, but I'm not the one making it. I think you also need spices and sweetness—the final elements and the ones with the most room for variability.

METHOD

What goes into chai is only half of it. There's also the ever-important *how*. Are we aerating the milk? Double boiling? Are the milk and water going in at the same time? Low boil or high? Do you steep the tea before adding the spices or do they all go in together? Does the sweetness come in the form of sugar before the boil, or is it honey at the bottom of an empty cup? Defining your method may sound overwhelming, but it's actually the most fun, if you ask me. This is where you get to really play around. Monitor the depth of the chai's tan as it steeps, use your nose to sense the balance of spices, take a quick sip to gauge the sweetness. You may enjoy the process just as much as the delicious end result.

RATIOS

In my opinion, the most defining ratio is milk to water. Since you steep the black tea in both at the same time, this ratio sets the tone for your chai. I personally use equal parts milk and water because I like my chai luxuriously creamy. Play with scaling the creaminess up or down to your liking.

MASALA

The other ratio to consider is the masala. With anywhere from three to twelve spices defining the chai masala, there's endless room for experimentation here. I prioritize ginger, cardamom, and fennel seeds over cinnamon, star anise, cloves, and black pepper, but, *again*, this is very personal.

Black pepper	Ground ginger
Cardamom	Mace
Cinnamon	Nutmeg
Cloves	Star anise
Fennel seeds	

Cue the Conversation

My approach to dinner party conversation is unique. It's not easy—or especially natural—to ask a group of eight-plus people to quiet down and listen to one person speak, but the benefits of doing it far outweigh any initial awkwardness you may feel when you first try it. Consider this my public plea for you to give it a try it at your next gathering. Open yourself up to new ways of connecting conversationally. Be a little vulnerable. Listen wholeheartedly. And share something you wouldn't normally.

The prompt really helps shape and steer this kind of conversation. It's a question that is asked of everyone, yourself included. I love to choose a question that's up for interpretation, so it takes some of the pressure off. Maybe you take it in a playful direction, or perhaps a purposeful one. In January, this can mean sharing a goal, your favorite cold-weather meal, or unmet resolutions of the past.

What's something people don't typically know about you?

What is a single decision you made that changed the trajectory of your life?

How do you define indulgence?

6 DAYS OUT

Prepare your shopping lists. I say *lists* plural because you're going to want to source from both grocers and your local farmers' market if possible. Go ahead and buy your long-shelf-life items, cross-referencing them with what's already in your pantry and spice cabinet. Save meats and produce until you're closer to your dinner party date. If you're open to making your own chaat masala, go ahead and create your spice mix and store it away.

5 DAYS OUT

Relax!

3 DAYS OUT

Shop for the rest of your ingredients, save for what you're planning to source from the farmers' market.

2 DAYS OUT

Marinate the chicken for Tandoori Chicken for 24 to 48 hours in the fridge.

Make your dressings for both the Quick-Pickled Carrot Salad and the Citrus Salad.

Go ahead and prep the dukkah for the carrot salad, storing it in an airtight container.

1 DAY OUT

Go to the farmers' market to get your produce and fresh flowers for the table. Be open-minded to substitutions while you're there! Nothing beats eating the best the farms have to offer us, even if it means the recipe changes a little.

Make the Apple Crisp. It reheats beautifully in the cast-iron.

Prepare the Raita and prep the crudités you've sourced. Clean your veggies and slice them into rough wedges, storing things like carrots in water to stay perky. The next day, all you have to do is pat them dry, plate the dish, and finish everything with a squeeze of lemon and flaky salt.

Set the table and pick your conversation prompt!

DINNER PARTY!

Start by making the Chana Masala and Fesonjoon. With their stew-like consistencies, they're very easy to reheat before you set the table.

Prep the citrus salad (but leave it undressed) and roast the carrots for pickling. Time will only aid the flavor of the carrots, so do not worry about doing this early.

I make the Tandoori Chicken and the Saffron Tachin last so that they're warm and not too dried out.

Don't forgot to reheat the Apple Crisp once dinner is winding down!

Valentine's Kitsch for Friends & Lovers

WITH JEN MONROE

Both chef and artist, Jen is incapable of being
boring. Her stylized, interactive, and thought-
provoking events under the moniker Bad Taste
push the boundaries of how we think about
food and consumption.

STEAL MY PLAYLIST

My friend Mariko introduced me to the idea of a group Valentine's Day dinner years ago. Not to be confused with Galentine's Day, group Valentine's Day dinner has nothing to do with your relationship status. Friends, lovers, exes, crushes are all equally welcome.

In a world (and on a day) when relationships can feel complicated, the message of this dinner party is simple: "Hey, I love you, eat this." In Mariko's version, a long table is stuffed into a friend's narrow gallery space. There may or may not be enough chairs for everyone, and it doesn't really matter, because people are intermittently standing and sitting and milling around all night, coming and going as they like. Food is dropped on the table on sheet trays, and it's beautiful yet unfussy, meant to be eaten with your hands. It might be ssambap with fresh leafy herbs, rice, grilled meat, and punchy sauces. There's probably a sheet of her legendary homemade focaccia with cheeses and pickles. Maybe someone brings a shellfish tower, and most everyone brings wine. For dessert, there are swan-shaped cream puffs with chocolate and fruit, which we assemble at the table. Casual, conversational, interactive, group Valentine's Day dinner is no less fueled by love than its traditional counterpart.

Ever since I first attended Mariko's party, I started riffing on this tradition and making it my own. My cooking style is a bit more involved, and I tend to inject loud colors into my food—and not just pinks and reds. Look forward to a whole fish encrusted in electric blue salt and violet-hued mashed potatoes. For me, colorful, unexpected food with over-the-top presentation is an ideal way to de-serious-ify Valentine's Day, to make it about joy, and to bring some brightness into the dead of winter.

When I design a menu, I include motifs I can repeat and interpret across recipes, like a melodic line reappearing in different movements of a jazz suite. One of the motifs you'll find at this dinner party is squiggles. The squiggle gives you exactly three opportunities to bust out your piping tips, because if not now, when? Grapes, pickles, and (surprise, surprise) heart shapes also make repeat appearances. Much of this food has a reliably retro sensibility: Piped mashed potatoes, for example, take their cue from duchess potatoes, a dish that gained traction in America in the mid-twentieth century. The deceptively simple two-ingredient absinthe cocktail is based on an Ernest Hemingway recipe. You could format the menu with a palate cleanser, which is a decidedly old-school fancy restaurant relic that I love (bonus points if you incorporate a finger bowl into your dinner!). The plating of the dessert course is inspired by one of my favorite old cookbooks—*The Romance of Food*—by the prolific romance novelist Barbara Cartland, and her aesthetic fingerprints are all over this dinner. You'll also notice a deliberate lack of chocolate, because even though I am a chocolate lover, nobody needs to see another chocolate-covered, out-of-season strawberry in the middle of February. This is a thoughtful, kitschy meal that is equal parts beautiful and silly: It doesn't take itself too seriously, because hosting shouldn't be a serious ordeal.

Lastly, a reminder that making eight different recipes for a dinner party (that you would also like to be present at) is very ambitious. Think of this menu as an open-ended template: Take what you like from it and ignore or repurpose the rest. I've also included lots of options to simplify and customize, and I hope you'll use them and have fun with them to make them your own. Invite your friends, your lovers, or both—what matters is that your food tells your guests that you love them.

Death in the Afternoon

Makes 1 cocktail

I love a simple, intense, deceptively chic old cocktail, and this one (adapted from So Red the Nose: or Breath in the Afternoon, *a collection of cocktail recipes) really delivers. The earliest known version of this recipe comes from Ernest Hemingway circa 1935, but I've dialed down his proportions because that thing is* boozy. *Hemingway calls for champagne, but it's my opinion that one shouldn't put very expensive wine in a cocktail, so I suggest using a good quality Cava, prosecco, or even a crémant, if you're feeling fancy. Avoid pét-nats, as they tend to go flat very quickly. If you'd like a lower ABV, substitute pastis for the absinthe, or knock the absinthe down to half an ounce.*

If you have any alcohol-free friends in attendance, there are a few simple things you can do to make them feel special. While a thoughtful iced tea or punch goes a long way, an even simpler solution is to make some beautiful ice cubes with edible flowers, herbs, or fruit suspensions inside for an instantly chic upgrade to a seltzer.

1 ounce absinthe

Cava, prosecco, crémant, or champagne, well chilled to top

Red or green grapes, for garnish (optional)

1. Pour the absinthe into a coupe or wineglass. Slowly pour in sparkling wine to fill. The drink will get beautifully cloudy.

2. If making the grape heart garnish, cut a grape in half on a diagonal. Flip one half of the grape and place cut sides together to form a heart. Skewer and place as garnish.

Pour One Out for Grandma

If I had to choose one word to describe my hosting sensibility, it would be "grandma." Specifically, a mid-century, sherry-swigging, blue eyeshadow–wearing grandma. This applies to drinks, too.

While amaro is the digestif du jour, there's plenty more grandma nightcap options ready to have their moment in the sun.

Try at Least One . . .

Cream sherry

Tawny port

Brandy

Sweet vermouth

Crème de menthe

Beet-Pickled Deviled Eggs

Makes 24 deviled eggs

It's a universal truth that most people love *deviled eggs, so what better to serve on the official day of love? And in honor of Valentine's Day, maybe those eggs should be a little pink? And maybe their yolks should be . . . piped into cute swirls with little flowers on top?*

12 large eggs (see Note)

Two 15-ounce cans sliced beets, undrained

2 cups white wine vinegar

½ cup sugar

3 teaspoons kosher salt, plus more to taste

1 tablespoon black peppercorns, lightly pounded

1 tablespoon yellow mustard seeds

1 teaspoon allspice berries

2 bay leaves

⅓ cup mayonnaise

1 teaspoon Dijon mustard, plus more to taste

½ teaspoon ground white pepper, plus more to taste

Pink food coloring (optional)

Edible flowers (optional)

Notes:
Hard-cooking very fresh eggs makes them exceedingly difficult to peel smoothly. Buy your eggs at least a week before you'd like to cook them and then the shells will pop off much more easily.

If you're piping your yolk mixture, you want very smooth yolks to avoid clogging the piping tip.

Make Ahead: The eggs can be removed from the pickle brine up to 2 days in advance. The yolk filling can be made up to 24 hours in advance; rebeat to soften prior to transferring to a piping bag.

1. Place the eggs in a heavy-bottomed pot and add cold water to cover by 1 to 2 inches. Bring to a rolling boil, turn off the heat, cover, and set a timer for 14 minutes. Prepare an ice bath.

2. When the timer goes off, remove the eggs from the water and place them in the ice bath. Let the eggs cool completely, then peel them and transfer to a large airtight container.

3. In a saucepan, combine the canned beets (including the liquid), vinegar, sugar, 2 teaspoons of the salt, the black peppercorns, mustard seeds, allspice berries, and bay leaves. Stir over low heat just until the sugar is completely dissolved; the mixture should be just barely warm. If it's too hot, let cool for a few minutes before pouring it into the container with the eggs. If it won't all fit, divide the eggs between two containers.

4. Cover and refrigerate for at least 12 hours or up to 3 days. The longer you leave them in the brine, the more pickled-tasting, pink, and firm they'll end up. For me, 24 hours is the sweet spot—you get a pretty pink gradient and nice flavor—but it's a personal preference.

5. Reserving the brine, remove the eggs and cut each egg in half. Scoop or pop out the yolks and place them in a medium bowl. Add the mayonnaise, mustard, white pepper, remaining 1 teaspoon salt, and 1 tablespoon of the reserved beet brine. Mix and mash with a fork until smooth (see Note). Taste and add additional salt, white pepper, or mustard as needed. If you'd like to add food coloring to tint your yolk mixture, add it now.

6. Either spoon the yolk filling into the eggs, or transfer the yolk mixture to a piping bag fitted with a large star tip. Pipe the filling in exaggerated mounds. Garnish with edible flowers (if using).

From East to the West
Sunshine Farms is the Best!
12 GRADE A
EXTRA LARGE EGGS
Stays Fresh
Happiness Inside Us!

Steamed Rose Buns

Makes about 18 buns

These are a fun pull-apart riff on Chinese steamed buns, or mantou, which are similar to bao but without filling. I like to use low-gluten Chinese bun flour, like mantou, which you can often find at Asian supermarkets. My personal favorite is Purple Orchid brand—it'll give you an extra-soft, fluffy bun—but cake flour or even all-purpose flour will give you a good result, too. I like to make the dough in a stand mixer with the dough hook, but you can definitely knead by hand instead. You can also play around with natural food colorings instead of gel paste (try turmeric or purple sweet potato powder). Serve with Molded Butter Candles (page 35) for dipping.

1 cup warm water

8 to 10 drops pink or red
  food coloring
  gel paste (optional)

1 tablespoon sugar

2 teaspoons active dry yeast

4 cups mantou flour, cake flour, or
  all-purpose flour

1 teaspoon baking powder

1½ teaspoons kosher salt

2 tablespoons unsalted butter,
  at room temperature

Mint leaves or other leaves,
  for garnish (optional)

Make Ahead: Let the buns cool completely before refrigerating in an airtight container for up to 3 days. Alternatively, you can flash-freeze the buns, uncovered and not touching each other, on a parchment-lined sheet pan or cutting board for 2 hours. Once they're frozen firm, put them in a freezer bag or airtight freezer-safe container. That first freezing step hardens them enough to prevent them from sticking together in the freezer bag (this is a great technique for freezing fragile things like cookie dough, meatballs, berries, dumplings, etc.). To serve, resteam the buns for a few minutes until soft and warmed through, or microwave in 10-second increments, covered in a damp paper towel, until hot and soft.

1. In a small bowl, combine the warm water, food coloring gel paste (if using), sugar, and yeast. Stir to dissolve and let stand until foamy, 5 to 10 minutes.

2. In a stand mixer fitted with the dough hook (or in a big bowl, if kneading by hand), combine the flour, baking powder, and salt. Add the yeast mixture and mix until it starts to come together (or by hand). If the dough is dry, add 1 tablespoon of water at a time until it comes together. Knead for 10 minutes, or until smooth, then add the butter. Knead until completely combined and smooth. Cover the bowl and let rest for 20 minutes.

3. Line bamboo steamer baskets with parchment paper or cabbage leaves. (If you have fewer than three baskets or are using your Always Pan steamer insert, you'll need to steam in multiple batches.)

4. Divide the dough in half and keep one half covered while you work on the other. Roll out on a lightly floured surface to a rectangle about 22 × 16 inches; the dough should be pretty thin. (If the dough is too tight and springing back too much to roll out, let it rest, covered, for 5 to 10 minutes so it can relax.) Using a 3½-inch round cutter or a similar size thin-rimmed drinking glass, cut as many rounds from the dough as you can.

5. Arrange a row of 4 halfway overlapping dough rounds. Use a small scrap of dough to roll a thin log about 3½ inches long. Set the log crosswise on the last dough round (the one on top) toward the edge of the round. Roll the dough rounds around the log to form a big cylinder. Cut the cylinder in half crosswise to form two rosettes. Gently open and shape the petal edges and place in your

(continued)

lined steamer baskets, leaving about 1½ inches space in between the buns. Keep the baskets covered as you continue to work on the rest of the dough. Repeat, rolling flowers until you've used all the dough rounds. Gather the remaining dough scraps into a ball and keep covered while you repeat the rolling and cutting steps with the second half of the dough. Gather all the remaining dough scraps into a ball, roll out, and punch out as many rounds as you can (this will be a much smaller batch).

6. Allow the buns to rest until slightly puffy, about 20 minutes.

7. Meanwhile, bring a pot with a few inches of water to a boil (or, if using your Always Pan steamer insert, bring a shallow layer of water to a simmer in the pan, checking that the water isn't touching the bottom of the steamer basket).

8. When the buns are ready, steam them, covered, over medium-high heat for 12 minutes. (Note: If you're using the Always Pan, you should cook at medium heat to ensure the water doesn't boil off.) After 12 minutes, turn the heat off and allow the buns to rest in the steamer, covered, for 5 minutes before removing the lid.

9. Serve warm, garnished with mint leaves to look like faux rose leaves if you like, with butter candles for dunking.

Molded Butter Candles

Makes as many candles as you want

Butter candles are a wonderful party trick that turn a humble ingredient into something that will make your guests lose their minds. Burning fat is the basis for a lot of candles (think whale blubber, oil, paraffin), so why not butter?

Serve a butter candle by lighting it, letting it melt down a bit, and then dipping bread (or vegetables, or popovers, or lobster, or whatever your heart desires) into the melty pools. I recommend using clarified butter, as it removes the water and milk solids from your candle, giving you a better burn and preventing the butter from separating into layers. (Also, if you've never cooked with or eaten clarified butter, get ready—it is SO delicious and luxe!)

For this dinner party, I go maximalist by tinting my butter light pink and molding it into a cherub shape, but there's lots of room to play here: You can try different colors or nix the tints all together; you can skip the candle wick and opt for a beautiful butter mold for slathering; you can try browning your butter for a nuttier flavor profile; and you can swap the mold out for a chic coupe glass, shallow bowl, or even an ashtray! If you'll be using a glass or ceramic vessel to serve your candle, I recommend using something broad and shallow that will be easy for your guests to dunk things in (i.e., not wineglasses, which tend to have a narrow opening).

Food-safe molds or vessels

Unsalted butter

Aromatics for infusing your butter (optional)

Food coloring (optional)

Cheesecloth or coffee filter (optional)

Food-safe wick, such as organic beeswax coated hemp wicks

Wooden or metal skewers

Kosher salt (optional)

1. Gather your molds, glasses, or whatever you'll be using for shaping your candles, and ensure that they're clean. Figure out how much butter you'll need by filling your vessels with water to the desired height, then pouring that water into a measuring cup. This is how much butter you'll need. Add a few extra tablespoons of butter to your quantity to account for what you'll lose in the cooking process. Dry out the interior of your molds or glasses very well.

2. In a heavy-bottomed saucepan (or a bigger pot, if you're making a lot of candles), melt the butter over medium heat. Once the butter is melted, add any flavoring aromatics (if using) and reduce the heat to low. Cook, stirring regularly and scraping the bottom of the pot. The butter will produce a white foam, which will eventually split apart and then begin to sink to the bottom. This means that the water is cooking off and the milk solids are separating (a good thing), though you don't want to

(continued)

scorch the milk solids, which is why this is over low heat. Once the bubbling activity has almost completely stopped, it means that the water has boiled off. Remove from the heat.

3. If you've used any flavoring aromatics, pour the whole mixture through a fine-mesh sieve to remove them. Discard the aromatics or reserve for another use. If using any food coloring, add it now. To remove the milk solids, you can then either strain your butter mixture through several layers of cheesecloth or a coffee filter, or take the lazy method (my favorite): Pour your butter into a clear, tall container and let it sit for about 10 minutes. This allows the milk solids and any leftover bits to sink—you should see a layer of sediment settled at the bottom. Carefully and slowly, pour the butter into your molds or vessels, watching to make sure none of the sediment layer gets into your candle. If the sediment starts to get mixed into the butter as you're pouring, simply let it sit for a minute or two so it settles down again, and resume pouring.

4. If you're making your candle in a coupe glass or similar, skip to the next step. If you're using an intricate or detailed mold, place it in the freezer for at least 4 hours. You want your butter to be frozen solid so that it can pop out of the mold easily without breaking. After unmolding, refrigerate for at least 8 hours to let the butter thaw before you add your wick.

5. To add a wick, use a sturdy skewer to drill a vertical hole through the top center of your mold, going all the way down to the bottom. (If your butter cracks a bit from the skewer, don't worry—you can gently and quickly press the butter back together.) Remove the skewer and insert your food-safe wick into the hole as deep as possible. Trim the top of the wick to about ⅓ inch high.

6. To serve, bring the candle to room temperature if you'd like it to melt faster, or serve it straight from the fridge if you'd like a longer burn. Light it at the table, sprinkle it with salt if desired, and serve with whatever your heart desires.

Make Ahead: Finished candles will last for months in the fridge or freezer. Store in an airtight container or wrap tightly to prevent butter from absorbing any odors.

Scallop & Grape Ceviche

Serves 8

This is a very sensuous, Botticelli-esque appetizer. Buttery slices of scallops take a bath in magenta-hued aguachile, with fiery heat that's kept in line by silky coconut water and cucumber. Floral sanshō pepper adds a beautiful perfume and a drizzle of scallion oil adds a savory richness. This recipe is a great opportunity to make a trip to your local fishmonger. Not only is their product better than supermarkets, but you can talk through any questions you might have, if this is your first time working with scallops. While you won't be cooking these with heat, the acidic lime juice "cooks" the scallops in this dish.

2 bunches of scallions

1½ cups neutral oil, such as peanut, vegetable, or corn

1½ pounds large dry-packed sea scallops

2 cups fresh lime juice (18 to 20 limes)

⅓ cup coconut water

½ large English cucumber, peeled

½ habanero pepper, with seeds, plus more to taste

½ teaspoon ground sanshō pepper, plus more to taste

1 teaspoon kosher salt, plus more to taste and for serving

½ teaspoon powdered pitaya (dragon fruit), for color (optional)

Crushed ice, for serving (optional)

Extra-large scallop shells, for serving (optional)

½ cup green grapes, sliced crosswise

Black sesame seeds

Make Ahead: Scallion oil can be made 2 weeks ahead and kept refrigerated. The aguachile can be made without the lime juice 1 day in advance, then add the lime juice once the scallops have been marinated in it and proceed as written.

1. Trim the scallion ends and cut off the white parts, leaving just light and dark green parts. Reserve the whites for another use.

2. In a blender, blend the scallions and oil together until as smooth as possible, 1 to 2 minutes. Pour the mixture into a saucepan, bring to a gentle simmer, and cook for 10 minutes. Taste. If the oil doesn't have a pleasant scallion flavor yet, cook a few minutes more. Remove from the heat and let cool for 5 minutes before straining the mixture through a clean kitchen towel. Twist and wring the towel to squeeze out the remaining oil. (The oil will be hot, so be careful and wear gloves, or use tongs if needed!) Discard the scallion solids, transfer the oil to a squeeze bottle, and let cool completely. The oil will keep in the refrigerator for a few weeks.

3. If the scallops still have tough abductor muscles attached, remove and discard them. Pat the scallops dry and slice into fat coins. Place in a medium bowl. Pour the lime juice over them, tossing to make sure everything is coated. Cover with a lid or plastic wrap and refrigerate for 30 minutes, tossing once halfway through.

4. To make aguachile, in a blender, combine the coconut water, cucumber, habanero pepper, sanshō pepper, and salt and blend until smooth. Taste. The mixture should have an assertive heat to it since it will be diluted with lime juice later on. Add more sanshō pepper, salt, and/or habanero if desired. Add the pitaya powder

(if using) and blend again. The pitaya powder is primarily for color, so if you'd like it to be a darker pink, add a bit more and blend until you're satisfied with the both the color and flavor. Refrigerate the mixture in an airtight container until ready to use. (If you're proceeding with the rest of the recipe right away, you can refrigerate it in the blender jar.)

5. When the scallops are done marinating, they should be pretty opaque. If they are still translucent, let them marinate an additional 10 minutes, or as needed. When they are done, drain and reserve the lime juice. Add ⅓ cup of the reserved lime juice to the aguachile and blend. Taste again and adjust for final seasoning. The liquid should be limey, spicy, well salted, and a pink color that you're happy with, so adjust as needed.

6. To assemble the ceviche, fill serving plates with crushed ice. (A wide, shallow bowl like the Midi Bowl works great here.) Nestle the shells into the ice so they're relatively stable and won't spill. (Note: If you'd rather skip the ice and the shells, serve the ceviche in small plates or bowls of your choosing.) Pile coins of sliced scallop into the shells, then tuck the grape slices in between the scallop pieces so they peek out. Carefully pour the aguachile into the shells. (I like to pour around the edges of the shell so the scallops remain clean and are nested in the liquid.) Garnish with a very light smattering of black sesame seeds, dots of scallion oil, and an additional sprinkling of salt. Serve immediately.

Mashed Purple Potatoes

Serves 8

There are a handful of different purple potato varieties, such as Peruvian purples and Magic Molly, and they'll all work great here, but avoid purple Japanese sweet potatoes, which are too sweet for an application like this. Also, if you're using very small potatoes, you'll want to scale the quantity up an extra ¾ pound to make up for the weight you'll lose in peeling them.

1¾ cups whole milk, plus more as needed

12 garlic cloves, halved lengthwise

1 tablespoon black peppercorns, lightly crushed

14 tablespoons (7 ounces) unsalted butter

Peel of 1 lemon, in wide strips

1 bay leaf

Kosher salt

4 pounds purple potatoes (see Headnote)

1 teaspoon ground white pepper

Fresh herbs, lemon slices or curls, canned pearl onions or Holland onions, edible flowers (all optional)

Make Ahead: The potatoes can be made up to 3 days ahead. Transfer to an airtight container, uncovered, and let cool completely at room temperature. Cover and refrigerate. Reheat over medium heat, whisking, and loosening with additional milk as needed.

1. In a medium pot, combine the milk, garlic, peppercorns, butter, lemon peel, bay leaf, and 2 teaspoons salt and bring to a simmer. Immediately turn off the heat, cover, and let steep for at least 30 minutes.

2. Peel the potatoes, dropping them into a large pot of cold water as you work. (Note that if you're using a ricer, you can skip peeling.)

3. Drain the water from the potato pot and replace with a generous covering of cold water. Salt the water well and bring to a boil. Cook until the potatoes are very tender and a paring knife goes in with almost no resistance. The timing will depend on the size of your potatoes, but you can start checking them after 10 minutes of boiling.

4. Drain the potatoes and, while still hot, press them through a ricer back into the pot.

5. Check the milk mixture. If the butter has solidified at all, give it a quick reheat. Strain the mixture into a measuring cup, discarding the solids. Add about two-thirds of the mixture to the potatoes along with the white pepper and stir to combine. You want a mash that is soft enough to pipe but that will still hold its shape (i.e., not soupy or stiff). If it's too thick, continue adding more milk mixture until the desired texture is achieved. Taste for seasoning and adjust as needed.

6. Shortly before you're ready to serve, transfer about two-thirds of the mash to a serving bowl. Place the rest in a piping bag fitted with a large star tip, or tip of your choosing. Pipe designs onto the surface of the potatoes and decorate with any garnishes you choose. If you need to hold the piped potatoes in a low oven for a few hours, carefully tent with foil to prevent drying out and preserve your design. Reserve any fragile or wiltable garnishes, like fresh herbs or flowers, until right before serving.

Whole Salt-Roasted Fish

Serves 6 to 8

Say hello to a highly customizable, tasty, and borderline ridiculous (in a good way) showstopper of a main course. If you're unfamiliar with salt-roasting, fear not: This will not make your fish unpalatably salty. Instead, the salt crust exterior's primary function is to tightly seal in moisture, so the fish is effectively steaming itself and intensifying the flavors of the aromatics you've stuffed inside. The salt crust and fish skin are removed after baking, leaving beautifully moist and perfectly seasoned meat behind.

Many salt-baked fish recipes call for using egg white as a binding liquid for your salt mixture, but I find water works just fine. This means that if you choose to tint your salt a fun color, as I've done here, the color will hold beautifully in the oven. I used phycocyanin, a brilliant blue type of spirulina powder, but you can use the turquoise kind of spirulina, turmeric, beet powder, or even activated charcoal.

If you've never salt-roasted a fish before, I strongly recommend trying it out on a smaller fish before making it for a crowd so you can get comfortable with the technique. It's fairly straightforward but can be a bit messy, and you'll need to be very careful when taking the salt crust off so as to not get any inside the fish's cavity. When making it for a group, I like to take the salt crust off at the table so everyone gets to see the whole fish, and then bring it back to the kitchen to dispose of the salt crust, remove the fish skin, and separate the fillets from the bones, because I get nervous when people are watching me. But if you'd rather cut everything at the table and have it be a fun, messy, dramatic tableside experience, you do you.

Fresh herbs and aromatics of your choosing, such as ½ lemon cut into thin slices, a few crushed garlic cloves, coins of fresh ginger, or any combination of parsley, cilantro, chives, basil, dill, or tarragon

1 whole fish (3 pounds), such as red snapper, bass, branzino, dorade, or trout, scaled and gutted

Extra-virgin olive oil

3 pounds coarse kosher salt, such as Morton (avoid Diamond Crystal, which is too fine)

2 teaspoons blue spirulina/phycocyanin (optional)

Pink and black peppercorns, for garnish (optional)

Lemon wedges and fresh herbs, for garnish and serving (optional)

1. Preheat the oven to 400°F. Line a sheet pan with parchment paper.

2. Stuff the desired aromatics inside the cavity of the fish. Brush both sides of the fish exterior with a generous coating of olive oil.

3. In a large bowl, combine the salt, ¾ cup water, and the spirulina (if using) and mix well to combine. The mixture should be evenly damp like wet sand. Add a bit more water if needed, or drain any excess if it's puddling at the bottom. Place a layer of salt mixture about ½ inch thick and slightly larger than the fish (not including the tail) on the lined pan.

4. Place the fish on top of the salt bed. Begin packing salt on the top and sides of the fish in a layer at least ½ inch thick, leaving the head

area and tail uncovered. Once the body is done, place an instant-read digital thermometer into the thickest part of the fish (about 2 inches behind the eye is a safe bet). Now, pack the salt around the head while leaving the thermometer in the fish. When you've finished packing the salt, take the thermometer out: You've just created a hole that you can use later to check the temperature without cracking the salt crust open.

5. If using any garnishes for the exterior, apply them now. I used pink peppercorns to make a dot pattern and then used a big black peppercorn for the eye. You can also use the edge of a spoon to indent a scale pattern into the salt. Note that if you use any citrus or herbs on the outside, they'll get very brown in the oven. Make sure that your thermometer hole is still visible and open before putting the fish in the oven.

6. Bake for 30 minutes and then check the temperature using your thermometer hole. The fish should be 130°F. If needed, roast for an additional 5 to 15 minutes to attain the correct temperature.

7. Let the fish rest for 5 minutes and then use a knife to cut along its top side (not the side where its belly cavity is). Carefully remove and discard the salt crust, brushing away any lingering salt and taking care not to get any salt crust into the cavity. Now remove and discard the skin, which should peel off easily. Use a spatula to remove the fish fillets, feeling to get in between the bones and the flesh in order to leave the bones behind. If you're doing this tableside, you can serve the fillets directly onto your guests' plates, or pile them onto a serving plate. When one side of the fish is done, flip it over and repeat, removing the skin first.

8. If desired, serve the fish with lemons for squeezing and garnish with additional fresh herbs.

Roses Are Dead

Don't feel up to doing a whole floral thing? Buy cheap carnations (a deeply misunderstood flower) from the deli, trim their stems short, and stuff them into a vintage glass or crystal candy dish. Or skip the dish altogether, and cut the stems off the carnations and scatter them directly onto the table. Done and done.

Hot Potato Handwarmers

Compelling, right? These are . . . exactly what they sound like, and they work best if you live somewhere that is cold in February.

1. Count the number of hands that will be in attendance at your party. Subtract any that will be sleeping over.
2. Acquire said number's worth of hand-size potatoes (at least the size of a golf ball, but not so big that they will take up an entire coat pocket).
3. Boil or bake them until they're cooked through, about 30 minutes depending on the tater's size.
4. Keep them warm in a low (250°F) oven until it's time to part ways with your guests.
5. Carefully wrap them in a layer or two of muslin or cheesecloth and give them to your guests on their way out.
6. Pro tip: Remind your guests that they can repurpose their handwarmers as breakfast potatoes the morning after.

Genmaicha Pavlova with Meyer Lemon Curd Chantilly

Serves 8

Since the main course of this menu is family-style, I like to take advantage of the last course to do some really over-the-top individual plating. Pavlova is one of my all-time favorite desserts. I love its wild combination of textures: a shattery meringue exterior with a pillowy interior, buttery curd, fluffy whip, and juicy fruit. This one is a little bit extra, and you can, of course, adjust it to your preferences. Powdered genmaicha tea (Japanese green tea with toasted brown rice) in the meringue base lends a gorgeous toasty savoriness to balance the sweetness, but you can swap in a different powdered tea or flavor extract, or skip it altogether.

I also really love acidic, punchy desserts, so I've included two acidic elements here: curd and passion fruit goo. Since Meyer lemons are less acidic than conventional lemons, this isn't an aggressively sour curd, which is why I've upped the ante with passion fruit. If you don't love sour or don't have access to fresh passion fruit pulp, you could go with one or the other rather than both. Either way, I recommend going very light on the passion fruit pulp, as it can be quite intense, and you don't want to drown out all the other flavors.

This is a great place to show off winter fruits, so use what you have access to and what you love to eat. Poached quince would be beautiful here, as would many of the exotic citruses that show up in the winter.

Meringue

1 tablespoon cornstarch

1 cup sugar

½ cup egg whites, at room temperature (reserve yolks for the curd)

¼ teaspoon cream of tartar

¼ teaspoon kosher salt

1 teaspoon pure vanilla extract

2 tablespoons finely ground genmaicha tea (optional)

Lemon Curd

1 stick (4 ounces) unsalted butter

2 tablespoons grated Meyer lemon zest

½ cup fresh Meyer lemon juice

¾ cup sugar

½ teaspoon kosher salt

4 large egg yolks

Assembly

1 cup heavy cream, well chilled

1 teaspoon vanilla extract

¼ teaspoon kosher salt

8 ounces passion fruit pulp (optional; see Note)

Fruit of your choosing, cut into bite-size pieces

1. Make the meringue: Position racks in the upper and lower thirds of the oven and preheat the oven to 275°F. Line two baking sheets with parchment paper or silicone baking mats.

2. In a small bowl, whisk the cornstarch into the sugar.

3. In a stand mixer fitted with the whisk, whip the egg whites, cream of tartar, and salt together, starting on low and increasing the speed incrementally to medium. Beat until the mixture holds soft peaks and the egg white bubbles are very small and uniform, 2 to 3 minutes.

(continued)

4. Increase the speed to medium-high and gradually, slowly, add the sugar/cornstarch mixture. Continue to beat until glossy, stiff peaks form when the whisk is lifted, about 4 minutes. The mixture should be very thick. In the final moments of beating, add the vanilla and genmaicha (if using).

5. If you'd like to pipe your meringue into heart shapes, fit a piping bag with a large star tip. Transfer the mixture to the piping bag and pipe 8 hearts about 4 inches tall by 4 inches wide at their widest onto the baking sheets. It helps to pipe each heart in a single layer, and then pipe a second layer on top only around the edges, creating a hollow in the center of the heart that you will later be filling with tasty things. (Alternatively, use two spoons to drop 8 rounded blobs onto the baking sheets, creating small craters in the center of each with the back of a spoon.)

6. Transfer the baking sheets to the oven and reduce the oven temperature to 250°F. Bake for 20 minutes and then switch racks and rotate the baking sheets front to back. If the meringues appear to be cracking or taking on too much color, reduce the temperature by another 25°F. Bake until the meringues are crisp and dry to the touch on the outside, about another 20 minutes, although the insides may still feel quite soft (they should still be white). If the outsides feel too wet or soft, bake for up to 20 minutes more, taking care not to overbake, as they will firm up as they cool.

7. When they're done, turn the oven off, crack the oven door open, and leave the meringues to cool inside. Cooling them slowly helps prevent cracking and collapsing. Once completely cooled, gently peel the meringues off the parchment or silicone mats and transfer to an airtight container for storage.

8. Make the lemon curd: In a heatproof bowl set over a medium-heat saucepan of simmering water (the bottom of the bowl should not touch the water), melt the butter. Stir in the lemon zest, lemon juice, sugar, and salt. Reduce the heat to low and add the egg yolks, whisking continuously over the simmering water until thickened. This will take about 10 minutes.

9. To assemble: In a bowl, with an electric mixer (or by hand with a whisk), beat the heavy cream, vanilla, and salt until it creates soft peaks.

10. If using the passion fruit pulp, spread a thin puddle of it on each plate. Note that this should be a very sparse layer of pulp to avoid an overpowering flavor.

11. Place a meringue heart on top of the passion fruit pulp and spoon about a tablespoon of the lemon curd into the center. Top with a very generous dollop of whipped cream, and then garnish with prepared cut-up fruit of your choosing. Serve immediately.

Note: If using the pulp of fresh passion fruit, gut all of the fruits into a bowl and then give it a good stir to break up any globs. To get the amount needed here, you'll need to buy 8 to 10 passion fruit.

Make Ahead: Meringues can be stored in an airtight container for up to a week in a low-humidity environment. Lemon curd can be refrigerated for 2 to 3 weeks or frozen for up to a year. Fruit garnishes can be sliced and refrigerated several hours in advance.

Find Your Valentine's (Mis)match

I like to source cheap, colorful vintage glass or crystal pieces online (mismatching highly encouraged) to repurpose for dessert, drinks, or even flowers.

JEN'S SEARCH TERMS

Vintage
"Vintage compote" "Vintage candy dish" "Vintage sherbet glasses" "Vintage cabbage bowls"

Bonus: **"Antique swan salt cellar"** A frivolous but highly covetable table accessory. You're welcome.

Prep lists are your best friend. Spreading prep out in smaller blocks across as many days as possible will help prevent cooking fatigue and make the day of your party feel way more manageable. Once you've settled on a menu, figure out which elements can be pushed to when, write out a schedule day by day, and stick to it! Note that the following schedule assumes you're making all these recipes, which is a lot for an at-home party, so please remember to make however much of this menu feels manageable for you and leave the rest for another time.

6 DAYS OUT

Make your shopping list and get everything except seafood and any super-perishable fruit or edible flowers. (And as a reminder, you'll want to buy eggs for deviled eggs at least a week before cooking.)

Make the butter candles, refrigerating when complete.

5 DAYS OUT

Bake the meringues for the pavlovas, storing at room temperature in an airtight container once completely cooled.

4 DAYS OUT

Make the lemon curd for the pavlovas, storing in the fridge in an airtight container.

3 DAYS OUT

Make the Steamed Rose Buns, refrigerating in an airtight container once completely cooled.

Hard-cook, peel, and pickle the eggs for the deviled eggs.

2 DAYS OUT

Make the mashed potatoes and store in the fridge.

Remove the eggs from the brine and store in the fridge in an airtight container.

1 DAY OUT

Cut the eggs and make the yolk filling mixture. Store separately in the fridge in airtight containers.

Make the aguachile for the ceviche, but hold off on the lime juice.

✳ DINNER PARTY!

Fill and assemble the deviled eggs.

Cut the fruit and whip the cream for the pavlovas.

Add the lime juice to the aguachile and complete the ceviche.

Resteam the rose buns.

Reheat and assemble the mashed potatoes.

Make the Whole Salt-Roasted Fish.

Make cocktails to order.

A Goodbye Party for Winter

WITH LAUREN SCHAEFER & AMIEL STANEK

This Hudson Valley–based couple would rather be in the
kitchen together than just about anywhere else. Lauren
is a chef who has run restaurants, cooked events big and
small, and worked as a food stylist on *all kinds* of projects;
Amiel writes and edits stories about food and cooking,
mostly for *Bon Appétit*. They often fall asleep talking about
what they're going to make for dinner the next night.

March can be . . . a challenging month in the Hudson Valley. The days are short. The skies are gray. The trees and fields are bare. Spring is, technically speaking, just around the corner—but we'll believe it when we see it.

STEAL MY PLAYLIST

Until then, the only sane thing to do is embrace winter in all its glory and gather people for a long, lazy dinner party that leans into the hearty, braisey beigeness of it all. Good food and good company make the season make sense.

This is the ideal time for a menu that requires a little more advance work than we're inclined to do in the warmer, busier days ahead. The same way that spring and summer are all about barely touched peak-season produce and quickly cooked proteins, winter cooking at its best involves taking the time to coax extraordinary flavor from humbler raw materials. We're trying to find ways to celebrate the limited palette of the local ingredients we have at our disposal, to treat this occasion like a going-away party for all those knobby storage vegetables and braising cuts. With a little love, they'll shine just as brightly as any plate of sliced August tomatoes or salt-and-pepper steak. So, yes, this means that we're spending a lot of time in the kitchen leading up to a dinner like this. (It literally cannot be done in one day, so don't even try.) We spread out the work over a week (or more, in the case of some dishes), carving out a few hours here and there so we never feel rushed. What better way to spend our time? The kitchen is to winter what the swimming hole is to summer: The Place to Be.

Another organizing principle of this menu: We want this dinner party to last. This is not an arrive-at-7-leave-at-10 affair. It's a Big Hang, the kind that starts well before the sun goes down and wraps up when everyone is nodding off on the couch. (It's March—nobody has anything to do anyway.) Food and drink set the pace, which should feel loungey and elastic. Crudités and pork rillettes and bread are set out before the first guests arrive, just a little something to help everyone ease in and alleviate the anxiety of anyone who showed up hungry. This creates a bubble of time wherein proper hosting can happen. Coats are hung. Cocktails are made. Wine is chilled. People can sprawl out and relax.

Then, once everyone is spread and settled, the real fun starts. You can sneak into the kitchen and return with a flaming round of gooey cheese—everyone loves a little theater. You can pass around bite-size pieces of griddled sandwiches stuffed with briny anchovies—salt makes everyone drink more. You can wait until everyone is full of snacks to pop a hearty, one-pan braise into the oven—they'll be hungry again in an hour or so, don't worry. And when the main course does emerge, the party coalesces like magic—everyone was everywhere, and now they're around the table, mellow and eager and in peak form.

And that's where they'll stay. For bowls of hot sauerkraut and meat ladled over steaming rice. For a lemon dessert that everybody says they don't have room for but they obviously do. For a digestif (or two, or three) from a serve-yourself tray of bottles that's just too inviting to say no to. Crescendo, decrescendo. People leave if they have to, stay if they want, puddle on the couch if they're very drunk, or help tidy if they're very kind. It's the kind of evening that could only happen right here and right now—and makes right here and right now something to be grateful for.

Anatomy of a Digestif Tray

There are many reasons why someone might turn down the offer of an after-dinner drink. Maybe they don't want to be an imposition. Maybe they don't know what they like. Maybe they feel awkward that they might be the only person who says yes. Setting out a well-stocked tray of bottles and accoutrements obviates all these concerns, and creates the kind of inviting, convivial, appropriately inebriated atmosphere you're after.

Something Brown
Bourbon. Scotch. Rye. Cognac. Something dark and high-octane for the folks who believe no great meal would be complete without it.

Something Bitter
An amaro is nonnegotiable, a true digestif if there ever was. We love Braulio, Fernet-Branca, and Averna.

Something Clear
Eau-de-vie, unaged brandy, schnapps, and other clear spirits are potent and clarifying, capable of cutting through the most languorous of food comas. Mezcal is good here, too.

Something Sweet
In addition to being just generally delicious, sweet vermouths, aperitif wines, ports, and wines with a bit of residual sugar are very civilized (and approachable) ways to round out dinner.

Something Hot
A pot of uncaffeinated tea, tisane, or even just some hot water with a bit of lemon peel and sliced ginger should always make an appearance, be it for teetotalers or those who have had too much.

Accoutrements
Stacks of glasses that can work with both hot and cold drinks. A bowl of ice. Strips of lemon peel. A bottle of sparkling water for anyone who wants to elongate their drink. A few inviting oranges, a dish of almonds, and a broken bar of chocolate wouldn't be bad either.

Spätlese Spritz

Makes 1 drink

We absolutely love Riesling, and maybe the sweeter types like Spätlese and Auslese most of all. These wines get a bad rap, usually because people have only experienced cheap examples of them. But the genuine article has so much more than sweetness to offer. There's lots of acidity hiding under that residual sugar, which makes them especially refreshing and mouthwatering. Still, sweet wines can be a bit of a hard sell, which is why we like to combine them with Zubrowka—a Polish vodka infused with native bison (or vanilla) grass—and tonic water for an easy-drinking cocktail that highlights the Riesling's more floral qualities. If you're making these for a crowd, combine the Riesling and vodka in a pitcher ahead of time in the same 2:1 ratio—that way, all you have to do is measure 3 ounces of the booze mixture and 3 ounces of tonic for each cocktail.

Ice
1 ounce Zubrowka or any kind of vodka
2 ounces Spätlese or Auslese Riesling
3 ounces tonic water
Lemon peel

1. Fill a wineglass with ice, then add the Zubrowka, Riesling, and tonic water and stir briefly to mix.

2. Express the lemon peel over the top of the cocktail, rub it around the rim of the glass, then plop it right into the drink.

Anchovy & Scallion Toasties

Serves 8

Okay, yes, these are just little grilled cheese sandwiches filled with salty anchovies and sliced scallions. But served in the right context, there's absolutely nothing better. One such context: Cocktail hour turns into two or three, the party has naturally spread out—some people are in the kitchen, some are in the living room, some are at the table—and here you come, making the rounds with a platter of crispy, gooey little bites. Now that's hospitality! Another good context: You forget to make these before dinner, and make them for your latest-staying, drunkest guests. Also fun! One note about bread: While you might be tempted to use some kind of fancy sourdough Pullman loaf for this, it is really best with cheap, thinly sliced commodity white bread. Pepperidge Farm White Sandwich is the ideal, trust us.

8 slices white American cheese
8 thin slices white sandwich bread
One 3-ounce jar anchovy fillets in olive oil, drained
3 scallions, very thinly sliced
4 tablespoons (½ stick) butter, at room temperature

1. This may sound like a funny thing to say considering you're making grilled cheese sandwiches, but: Get your mise en place in order. Place a slice of cheese on each slice of bread and stack them up on a plate next to the stove. Spread out the anchovies on a plate and have the sliced scallions and butter in bowls ready to go.

2. Heat a two-burner cast-iron or nonstick griddle over medium-low heat. Add 2 tablespoons of the butter to the griddle and spread it around so it coats the surface evenly. Place 4 of the cheese-topped bread slices on the griddle. Arrange 4 to 5 anchovy fillets on 2 of the slices, then sprinkle those slices with scallions.

3. Cook until the cheese is melted and the undersides are golden brown, 2 to 3 minutes. Flip the plain cheese-topped toast onto the anchovy-topped toast to make a sandwich and transfer the 2 sandwiches to a plate. Repeat with remaining butter, bread, cheese, anchovies, and scallions.

4. Cut each sandwich into triangles, arrange prettily on a plate, and serve immediately.

Playing with Fire

We're the kind of people who see the word "flambé" attached to something on a menu and order it immediately—is there anything more fun than watching someone set your food on fire? While this technique feels very restauranty, it's really quite easy to do at home. The key is to have confidence, and to follow a few simple rules:

1. Use high-proof liquor (ideally 45% ABV or higher) like brandy, marc, Cognac, or rum.
2. Heat the liquor in a small pot or pan until just steaming before dousing food.
3. Make sure the food to be flambéed is on a heatproof surface, and well clear of anything flammable.
4. Tell everyone to stand back. Make sure they do! And then make sure to follow your own advice.
5. Use a long lighter or kitchen match to get everything started.
6. Always know where your fire extinguisher is (just in case).

Camembert Flambé

Serves 8

This is less of a recipe and more of a Good Idea—a casual wheel of cheese in flaming party clothes. Mushrooms accentuate the subtle earthiness of good camembert, but this will work well with whatever local camembert-style cheese you can get your hands on, or any small wheel of cheese for that matter. Even though the cheese is being heated up here, it's best to let it come up to room temperature on the counter for at least an hour or two so that it cooks more evenly. (We sometimes leave it out for days ahead of time so that it can ripen to its full potential.)

For the liquor to flambé the cheese, you can really use anything you'd be proud to drink so long as it is at least 90 proof (45% ABV). Use this as an excuse to buy yourself a nice bottle of something that you can serve as a digestif later.

One 8-ounce wheel camembert cheese

2 tablespoons olive oil

4 ounces shiitake, maitake, or oyster mushrooms, sliced or torn into bite-size pieces

Kosher salt

1½ ounces apple brandy

Crusty bread of your choosing (sourdough, baguette, crackers)

1. Remove the camembert from the fridge and let it come up to room temperature on the counter for at least 1 hour and up to 3 days. (The texture becomes gooier and the flavor richer the longer it sits out.)

2. Preheat the oven to 425°F.

3. In a small fry pan, heat the olive oil over medium heat until the oil begins to shimmer. Add the mushrooms and cook, stirring occasionally, until they're nicely browned, about 5 minutes. Season with a pinch of salt and cook for an additional minute or so, then transfer to a small bowl and set aside.

4. When you're ready to serve, transfer the camembert to a small heatproof dish or pan and cover with the cooked mushrooms. Transfer to the oven and bake until the cheese looks like it is just about to burst, 6 to 7 minutes. Pull from the oven and transfer to a trivet.

5. In a small saucepan, heat the brandy over medium-low heat just until bubbles start to form at the bottom of the pan, then pour it over the cheese. Make sure there's nothing flammable nearby, then quickly and carefully ignite the liquor with a match or long lighter. Wait until the flames disappear and serve immediately with bread.

Cellar Crudités with Parsley-Sesame Pesto

Serves 8

Years of painstakingly scrubbing and prepping breakfast radishes, pinky-size carrots, and other cutesy new-crop veggies for summer crudités platters have left us a little . . . jaded. So much work! Which is just one reason why working with chunky vegetables in the dead of winter is such a pleasure—there's just so much less peeling and slicing to do. But that's not all! Big kohlrabi, carrots, turnips, fat daikon, and green meat radishes that have spent months in a farm's walk-in fridge— they all boast robust, concentrated flavor and are uniquely delicious. We like to cut them into meaty, thumb-size chunks and treat them to the quickest blanch in super-salty water, which both seasons and softens them ever so slightly.

1 large bunch of parsley, tender leaves and stems, roughly chopped

¼ cup sesame seeds

1 cup grapeseed or sunflower oil

1 tablespoon toasted sesame oil

3 tablespoons rice vinegar or distilled white vinegar

2 garlic cloves

Kosher salt and freshly ground black pepper

Big, fat winter kohlrabi, carrots, turnips, daikon, and/or radishes

A lemon wedge

1. In a blender, combine the parsley, sesame seeds, grapeseed oil, sesame oil, vinegar, garlic, 2 teaspoons salt, and a few grinds of black pepper. Blend on high speed, pausing to scrape down the sides of the blender periodically, until the pesto is bright green and mostly smooth. Taste and add more salt and pepper if desired. Transfer the pesto to a bowl and refrigerate.

2. Bring a medium pot of water to a boil. Peel the vegetables and cut into thumb-size wedges. Season the blanching water generously with salt and stir to combine—it should be seawater-salty. Blanch the vegetables by the handful for about 30 seconds at a time, using a mesh spider or slotted spoon to transfer them to a sheet pan in between batches. Refrigerate the vegetables for at least 30 minutes.

3. To serve, place the bowl with pesto on a large platter or plate and arrange the crudités around the bowl. Squeeze lemon over the crudités and serve.

Make Ahead: Prepare the pesto up to 1 week before, storing in an airtight container in the refrigerator.

Choucroute Garnie a la Adobo

Serves 8

Alsatian choucroute garnie—basically a big braise of sauerkraut and mixed meats—is made for cold-weather entertaining. It's generous and pungent, filling and flexible, and easy to set up well ahead of time and pop in the oven when the time is right. Our version weaves in elements of the Filipino adobo Lauren grew up eating—lots of garlic, soy, and vinegar—which make for a saucy dish begging for plenty of plain, steamy white rice to soak it all up. The rice is nonnegotiable; the dish will seem far too salty otherwise.

3 pounds bone-in, skin-on chicken thighs

Kosher salt and freshly ground black pepper

2 tablespoons neutral oil

1 pound bacon, cut into 1-inch pieces

10 garlic cloves, thinly sliced

2-inch knob fresh ginger, peeled and cut into matchsticks

10 hot dogs, cut in half crosswise

2 quarts Gingery Sauerkraut (page 64) or store-bought plain lacto-fermented sauerkraut

1 cup soy sauce

1 cup apple cider vinegar

Cooked white rice, for serving

1. Preheat the oven to 375°F.

2. Season the chicken thighs generously on both sides with salt and pepper.

3. Add the oil to a 12- to 14-inch cast-iron pan and add the chicken thighs skin side down. Set over medium heat and let the chicken cook, undisturbed, until the skin is golden brown, 15 to 20 minutes. Transfer the chicken to a large plate and set aside.

4. Reduce the heat to medium-low and add the bacon, garlic, and ginger and cook, stirring often, until the garlic turns a pale golden color, 2 to 4 minutes. Transfer to another plate and set aside.

5. Add the hot dogs to the pan and cook, stirring occasionally, until browned on all sides, 4 to 6 minutes.

6. Add the sauerkraut, soy sauce, vinegar, bacon, garlic, and ginger and stir to combine, seasoning generously with black pepper.

7. Nestle the chicken thighs into the sauerkraut mixture skin side up so that they're nicely surrounded but not submerged.

8. Transfer the pan to the oven and bake until the sauerkraut mixture is bubbling and the chicken thighs are deeply browned, 25 to 30 minutes. Serve with rice.

Gingery Sauerkraut

Makes about 4 quarts

We're sauerkraut freaks. We almost always have a few quarts of kraut in the fridge and we add it to everything—soups, braises, salad dressings, sandwiches, rice bowls . . . you name it. And while we're fortunate to live in a time when quality, lacto-fermented sauerkraut is fairly easy to find, it's almost equally easy to make.

We often use a digital scale when making ferments like this for consistency's sake, but you don't need one. (If you want to use one, more power to you. Instead of adding salt by feel, simply weigh the vegetables, figure out what 2.5% of that number is, and add that much salt by weight.) As far as other additions are concerned, the world is your oyster. Caraway seeds. Coriander. Black pepper. Garlic. Chiles. We like this gingery version because it is a bit spicy and very versatile (and especially good with the Choucroute Garni a la Adobo on page 63), but feel free to go your own way. This recipe can easily be halved . . . or doubled.

5 pounds green cabbage
8 ounces fresh ginger
Kosher or sea salt

1. Remove any bruised or discolored outer leaves from the cabbage and cut into quarters through the core. Cut the cores out of each quarter and set them aside, then thinly slice or grate the cabbage, adding it to a large bowl as you go. (You want a bowl big enough to hold all the vegetables comfortably.) Trim the ends of the core chunks if they're woody and/or discolored, then thinly slice or grate the cores and add to the bowl.

2. Peel the ginger and finely chop, then add to the bowl with the cabbage. Toss in a generous 4-finger pinch of salt and start squeezing the cabbage as hard as you can to work the salt into it. Keep going until the cabbage starts releasing liquid and the shreds look wet and almost translucent instead of opaque. Give it a taste. It should be almost too salty, like McDonald's French fries; if it isn't, add more and go back to tossing and squeezing.

3. Walk away for a half hour or so to give your hands a break and let the sauerkraut get to know the salt more intimately, then give it another go. You'll know it is ready when the shreds are completely slack and soft and a good amount of liquid has collected in the bottom of the bowl.

4. Tightly pack the salted cabbage into a clean 1-gallon jar, ceramic crock, or food-grade plastic tub (nothing metal!). Add a handful at a time, pressing down firmly after each addition. Pour whatever liquid is left into the jar and press down firmly again—the cabbage should be totally submerged in the brine.

5. Use a clean plate or smaller jar filled with water to weight the cabbage down and keep it submerged, then cover the fermentation vessel with a clean kitchen towel to keep any bugs out, but allow airflow in and out. (Don't seal it with a jar lid at this point—the gasses produced in the

fermentation process need to escape!) Store the sauerkraut at room temperature, somewhere out of the way and out of direct sunlight.

6. Check on the sauerkraut every couple of days and give it a taste. Fermentation will happen more quickly in a warmer environment and slower in a cooler one, and how long you let the sauerkraut go is entirely up to you. The sweet spot in our house is usually around 2 weeks, at which point the flavor is pleasantly sharp and almost fizzy, but you might like it less or more funky. If you notice a bit of white growth on the surface of the kraut, don't worry—it's harmless, and can be scraped off and discarded if desired. If, on the other hand, you notice green, blue, black, or red mold, go ahead and pitch that batch.

7. Once the sauerkraut has fermented to your liking, transfer it to airtight containers that are easy to store in the fridge and keep it refrigerated—it will keep more or less indefinitely.

Root Vegetable Piccalilli

Makes about 4 cups

This root vegetable–based condiment is a riff on British piccalilli, a sweet-spicy relish that is no doubt inspired by South Asian chutneys. It's bracing, acidic, and crunchy, the perfect complement to rich cheeses and charcuterie like pâté or Pork Rillettes (page 66). Our version is raw and won't last as long in the fridge as a traditional piccalilli, but should still last the better part of a week. Serve leftovers alongside cooked meat, on a cheese plate, or layered onto a ham or turkey sandwich for a pop of acid and mustardy heat.

1 pound rutabaga, celery root, turnip, or a combination, cut into thin matchsticks

1 tablespoon kosher salt

⅓ cup rice vinegar

1 tablespoon Worcestershire sauce or soy sauce

3 tablespoons English mustard powder, preferably Colman's

2 tablespoons sugar

½ teaspoon ground turmeric

1 large shallot, finely chopped

2-inch piece fresh ginger, peeled and finely chopped or grated

1 apple, peeled and finely chopped

1. In a colander set over a bowl, toss the root vegetable matchsticks with the salt and set aside. Let sit for at least 1 hour and up to 3, tossing and massaging with your hands—gently at first, then more assertively as the pieces soften—to release liquid.

2. Meanwhile, in a medium bowl, whisk together the vinegar, Worcestershire sauce, mustard powder, sugar, and turmeric until well combined. Add the shallot, ginger, and apple and stir to combine.

3. Give the root vegetables one final squeeze to remove as much liquid as possible and add to the bowl with the dressing, tossing well to combine.

4. Pack the piccalilli tightly into a 1-quart container, pressing down to make sure the vegetables are mostly submerged, and refrigerate for at least 1 hour and up to 4 days.

Pork Rillettes

Makes about 4 cups

As far as charcuterie is concerned, this rustic confit pork pâté offers just about the best ease-to-impressiveness ratio out there. Time is the biggest input here—rillettes does not want to be rushed—and we would strongly advise against making it the same day you're planning on serving it. Rillettes tastes better as it sits and will last for weeks if stored under a layer of fat in the fridge. It's the ideal project for a lazy winter afternoon when having people over is still just an idea to look forward to. If you have a smaller guest count, this recipe can be halved easily.

2 pounds boneless
  pork shoulder

1 pound pork belly

12 ounces back fat, leaf lard,
  or rendered lard
  (non-hydrogenated)

4 sprigs fresh thyme

2 dried chiles de árbol or
  other small dried hot chiles

4 bay leaves

1 small cinnamon stick

Kosher salt

Crusty bread, cornichons,
  and/or Root Vegetable
  Piccalilli (page 65),
  for serving

1. Preheat the oven to 250°F.

2. Using a sharp knife, cut the pork shoulder and belly into roughly 1-inch pieces. If using back fat (and not lard), cut it into 1-inch pieces, too.

3. In a large Dutch oven or heavy ovenproof saucepan, combine the pork, back fat (or lard), thyme, chiles, bay leaves, cinnamon stick, and ½ cup water. Heat the mixture over medium-high heat until the water begins to bubble, stir, then transfer to the oven.

4. Cook, uncovered, stirring every hour or so, until the pork is extremely tender and falls apart when pressed with a spoon, 3½ to 4 hours.

5. Remove from the oven and allow to cool on the stovetop or counter until the mixture is still very warm but not too hot to touch.

6. Discard the woody thyme stems, chiles, bay leaves, and cinnamon stick. Carefully tilt the pan to the side and use a spoon to transfer about ¼ cup of rendered fat to a small bowl. Set the fat aside for later.

7. Using a wooden spoon or, better yet, a wooden pestle, mash the pork until finely shredded and no large chunks remain, adding generous pinches of salt and tasting as you go. Because the rillettes will be served cold or at room temperature, you want to make sure that the still-warm mixture is right on the edge of too salty; it'll taste just right when it cools.

8. Transfer the rillettes to your desired serving and/or storage vessels—making sure to pack it in tightly so there are no air bubbles—and top with the reserved rendered fat before covering and refrigerating. (We usually put half into a wide, straight-sided earthenware dish for serving and the other half into a plastic pint container.)

9. Remove from the fridge an hour or more before it is to be eaten, and serve with plenty of crusty bread, cornichons, and/or the root vegetable piccalilli.

Gooey Lemon Custard Cake

Serves 8

While we love to lean into the rich, braisey beigeness of the season, we wouldn't be able to get through winter in the Northeast without California citrus. And at the end of a long dinner party full of meat, cheese, and cellar vegetables, this bright, light dessert with peak-season fruit from warmer climes feels especially welcome. This cake is inspired by British puddings, and as it bakes, an airy cake layer rises up to hide gooey lemon custard. Splurge on fancy lemons if you can.

Softened butter, for the baking dish

3 large eggs, separated

1 tablespoon unsalted butter, at room temperature

1 cup plus 2 tablespoons granulated sugar

¼ teaspoon kosher salt

3 tablespoons all-purpose flour

Grated zest and juice of 2 to 3 small lemons (4 to 6 tablespoons)

1 cup whole milk

Powdered sugar, for dusting

Vanilla ice cream, salty nuts, winter citrus, dates, and your favorite digestifs

1. Preheat the oven to 350°F. Butter a 5-quart baking dish.

2. In a stand mixer fitted with the whisk, beat the egg whites at medium speed until stiff peaks form.

3. In a medium bowl, combine the butter, granulated sugar, and salt and use your hands to incorporate the butter into the sugar until the texture is like damp sand. Whisk in the flour, followed by the egg yolks, lemon zest, and lemon juice. Slowly whisk in the milk until fully incorporated.

4. Using a spatula, gently fold the beaten egg whites into the lemon/egg yolk mixture until just combined. Gently scrape the mixture into the prepared baking dish.

5. Bake until the cake is a light golden brown on top, 35 to 40 minutes. Dust with powdered sugar.

6. Serve warm or very cold with ice cream, and offer nuts, citrus, dates, and digestifs alongside.

This menu is, without a doubt, a bit on the elaborate side of things, and is impossible to do in one day. But it's also full of things that can not only be made ahead of time, but are better when they've had a bit of time to sit. Below, a guide to spreading out the work so you can actually enjoy your party.

UP TO 1 MONTH OUT
Make the Gingery Sauerkraut and store in airtight glass containers once fully fermented.

UP TO 2 WEEKS OUT
Make the Pork Rillettes and pack tightly into an airtight container.

3 DAYS OUT
Make the Root Vegetable Piccalilli and store in an airtight glass container.

2 DAYS OUT
Cut up the cellar vegetables for the crudités.

1 DAY OUT
Slice the mushrooms for the Camembert Flambé.
Make the Parsley-Sesame Pesto for the crudités.

✳ DINNER PARTY!
Cook the mushrooms for the Camembert Flambé.
Assemble the Camembert Flambé.
Blanch the cellar vegetables for the crudités.
Prep and assemble the Choucroute Garnie a la Adobo.
Bake the Gooey Lemon Custard Cake.

The Fullness of Spring

WITH MARYAH ANANDA

Culinary artist and model Maryah will tell you that she
is in the business of nourishment. Her cooking and
hosting style is informed by her curiosity and a belief in
food's spiritual and healing powers. She hosts to build
community and share her identity with others.

It recently dawned on me that the first dinner parties I ever attended were hosted at my house by my grandparents when I was a child. The foods they made—clear broth fish soups, fried meats with sticky rice, and lots of accompaniments like pickled mustard greens and papaya salad—were a stark contrast to the efficiency-first, long-shelf-life foods I normally had access to.

STEAL MY PLAYLIST

Despite the fact that I didn't eat big Laotian feasts on a nightly basis, these parties were the root of my culinary heritage and gave me the blueprint for the kinds of gatherings I am known for hosting today. They taught me that food is a language everyone speaks, and it's my favorite one to communicate in. When you're full—physically and spiritually—you are free to think about your dreams, open yourself to love, and have gratitude for the present moment. It's always an honor to get the chance to make my friends full with food, conversation, and togetherness. And what better time to capture that fullness than when the earth is waking up, seeds are turning to fruit, and the promise of abundance hangs in the air? April is just the beginning of spring's bounty—the market isn't overflowing in the way it is during the late summer months, but the season is full of promise and hope, which is exactly what I want to capture in my menu.

This dinner party is defined by flavor, freshness, ease, and interaction. The flavor comes naturally from the Lao-inspired recipes, cooking methods, and homemade sauces. The freshness arrives via a table full of raw local vegetables. The ease—I hope—is felt as you prep. The menu is designed to be accessible because I know how overwhelming hosting can feel at times. It's here to make planning pleasurable and bring some joy to your process. And lastly, the interaction happens at the crucial point when everyone comes together around the table to eat. This dinner party can be executed a couple of different ways, but regardless of whether you are plating or grazing, it is meant to be a tangible experience you share with others.

For it to be a proper dinner party in my eyes, people should eat with their hands. Our hands are vital tools that many believe—myself included—make the food taste better. It's a ritual that symbolizes togetherness and community. It enables us to be present, to experience the feel of the food as well as the taste, and be intentional as we build each bite. Wherever you are in the world, my hope is that throwing this dinner party will give you an excuse to go to your local market and feel what ingredients speak to you. It's my belief that everything can be substituted, and the best ingredients are the ones you have access to that inspire you. Much like our hands, the raw vegetables, herbs, and other accoutrements are integral utensils for this meal.

This chapter is unapologetically fish-forward. Fish is a delight best shared around a full table, which makes it the perfect excuse to throw a party. I present three distinct ways to prepare fish, and you get to choose which fish course will anchor your party. It is not the intention that you would make all three fish dishes! Rather, it is designed to give you agency over this dinner party, flexibility to talk to your fishmonger about what's freshest and most available that day, and what sounds yummiest to you, of course. Once you've chosen your fish, the rest of the menu (and table) is built around it. The vegetable spreads, salads, onigiri, and toppings all come together around the fish to create an inviting, grazeable, and customizable feast for your guests. From fridge and pantry staples you'll never regret having on hand to miso's surprising versatility to cooking seasonally, I hope these recipes make you feel confident in the kitchen and empowered to add your own spin on things. Play, discover, and find what brings you the most joy. So, let's get in tune with the intentions of nourishment and lean into the offerings of spring.

Start at the Top

Nothing makes me feel like I am able to throw a dinner party together on a whim quite like having a stocked pantry. Part of my home cooking practice involves me regularly making, stocking, and saving homemade sauces, toppings, condiments, dressings . . . all of it. When the "main ingredient" is a delicious green dipping sauce that pairs wonderfully with fresh cut vegetables (and that delicious green dipping sauce is already sitting prepped and ready in your refrigerator), you'll feel all the more empowered to host without the pressure. Plus, making your own pantry staples is so satisfying.

They're the kinds of things you're throwing on dishes morning, noon, and night, so even if you're just eating cold takeout leftovers, it adds a touch of that homemade quality that tastes so good. I like my table to be full of balance, so I include something crunchy, something green, something packed with umami, and something light to give people agency over every bite they take.

Yuzu Spritz

Serves 6

This yuzu spritz is literally the easiest and most delicious accompaniment to any dinner. It's fresh, light, and simple. It's so simple it barely needs a recipe! I love this because it adds to the ease of this dinner party yet yields joy and flavor. Use whatever yuzu juice brand looks good to you. You can find plenty of options at your local Asian grocer. I personally like Yuzuco.

Ice
Two 750ml bottles sparkling water
6 tablespoons yuzu juice
Simple syrup, to taste
6 lemon slices
Basil sprigs, for garnish (optional)
Edible flowers, for garnish (optional)

Fill 6 glasses with ice. Pour in sparkling water a little more than three-quarters of the way full for each glass. Add 1 tablespoon yuzu juice and 1 to 2 tablespoons simple syrup to each glass, along with 1 thin slice of lemon. Garnish each glass with a sprig of basil and/or 1 to 2 edible flowers, if desired.

Cronch Topping

Makes 4 cups

I consistently reach for all of these individual elements, so it just made sense to put them all into one delicious go-to topping. Fried garlic and shallot are in just about every Asian household—you can grab both of these easily at H Mart or your local Asian grocer. Sesame seeds are a staple, I love the crunch of store-bought fried soybeans, and ginger is one of the root flavors I build this recipe around. This is a crunchy universal topping that can literally go on anything. Soup, salad, stir-fry, grilled vegetables, yogurt, whatever you heart desires. Add it on top of lettuce wraps for a nice balance of crunch! Perfect to always have this on hand just like salt and pepper.

½ cup flaky sea salt
3 tablespoons grated lemon zest
1 cup fried garlic
1 cup fried shallots
1 cup fried soybeans
¼ cup black sesame seeds
¼ cup white sesame seeds
2 tablespoons ground ginger
2 tablespoons garlic powder
1 tablespoon red pepper flakes

1. Preheat the oven to 200°F. Line a baking sheet with parchment paper.

2. In a bowl, mix the salt and lemon zest. Spread on the lined baking sheet and bake until the citrus is dry, about 1 hour. Let cool completely.

3. In a bowl, combine the zest mixture, fried garlic, fried shallots, fried soybeans, both sesame seeds, ground ginger, garlic powder, and pepper flakes. Store in an airtight container for up to 1 month

Miso Citrus Dressing

Makes 4 cups

This dressing is beyond delicious and so simple. It'll keep in your fridge for about a month and is a perfect entry to the bright, sunny weather that comes with spring.

3 cups olive oil

5 tablespoons reduced-sodium white miso

Juice of 5 lemons (¾ cup)

2 teaspoons honey

In a medium bowl, combine the olive oil, miso, lemon juice, and honey. Use an immersion blender to mix until well incorporated. (Alternatively, thoroughly whisk until combined.) Store in an airtight container in the refrigerator for up to 1 month. It may separate in the fridge, so when ready to use, shake to recombine.

Universal Dipping Sauce

Makes about 3 cups

This sauce is very dippable—think dumplings, spring rolls—or can be lightly tossed in a salad, or even served on a grilled steak. It is so delicious, and it's a staple sauce that should be in your rotation. Use whatever fish sauce brand you know and love. My go-tos are Squid Brand and Golden Boy. I recommend making this at least a day in advance so that the flavors have a chance to mature and blend together. In a pinch, it's okay to whip this up last minute, but the flavors are better when left to sit.

1½ cups fish sauce

1 to 6 Thai chiles, depending on spice preference, thinly sliced with seeds

¼ cup sugar

6 garlic cloves, finely minced

¾ cup fresh lime juice (about 6 limes)

In a small bowl, whisk together the fish sauce, chiles, sugar, garlic, and lime juice until the sugar dissolves. Store in an airtight container in the refrigerator for up to 1 week.

The Best Green Sauce

Makes 4 cups

I developed this recipe by playing around. I threw all the ingredients into a blender and thought let's just see what happens. It has now become my go-to warm-weather sauce. It's creamy, zesty, fatty, and bright. In other words, a fantastic universal sauce!

1½ to 2 cups extra virgin olive oil

Two 7-ounce jars pitted Castelvetrano olives, drained

1 bunch of parsley

1 bunch of chives

1 bunch of fresh basil leaves

8 garlic cloves

2 teaspoons coconut aminos

Juice of 4 lemons (½ cup)

Sea salt

In a blender, combine 1½ cups of the olive oil, the olives, parsley, chives, basil, garlic, coconut aminos, and lemon juice and blend until completely combined. Slowly add more olive oil until you reach a super-smooth, creamy consistency. Taste and adjust the salt and acid levels with sea salt and lemon juice. Store in an airtight container in the refrigerator for up to 1 week.

Foundational Vegetable Accoutrements to Set the Table

I love the farmers' market. It's bustling, vibrant, and full of new produce and inspiration. Varieties of different lettuces, apples, beans, herbs, citrus . . . it is vast and bursting with life. When sourcing for this dinner party, I highly encourage you to make a trip to your local farmers' market. Let your senses guide you at the market. Smell and taste. Most important: Talk to the farmers and ask them what's best. Their knowledge of crops is a fantastic resource to tap into!

My dinner party table is always full of tiny bowls and plates filled with vegetables, fresh herbs, and big leafy greens that can act as cutlery should you choose. While this is a traditionally Laotian way of setting a meal, I wish all meals were served this way! Not only is the abundance of mini bowls beautiful, it helps facilitate a sense of community around the table, anchoring the table and encouraging interaction. And you can create something new each time you go back for more. Here's how I like to group my vegetables and think of creating balance on the table. By no means do you need to include all of these, but try to select a couple from each group.

THE BASICS	KEEP BUILDING	ADD A SURPRISE
Cucumbers	Watermelon radish	Garlic scapes
Cilantro	Turnips	Broccoli flowers
Basil	Asparagus	Oyster mushrooms
Scallions	Kohlrabi	Chive flowers
Butter lettuce		Purple shiso leaves
Radicchio		

Umami Salad

Serves 6

This salad combines the elements of a perfectly constructed lettuce cup bite: zest, fresh lettuces, crunch, and earthiness, and works especially well paired with fried or grilled fish. This salad, with its slight sweetness and zippy brightness, is the embodiment of spring. Personally, I love to eat it all by itself outside the context of the dinner party. My favorite setting to eat this salad? Sitting cross-legged on a sunny balcony, soaking in the first rays of sun season.

2 medium daikon radishes, peeled and cut into thin half-moons

3 Asian pears, quartered and thinly sliced

2 cups Muscat grapes

1 medium head radicchio Rosa, cored and leaves separated

1 medium head Castelfranco radicchio, cored and leaves separated

1 cup Miso Citrus Dressing (page 76)

Olive oil, for drizzling

Juice of 1 lemon

3 bunches of chives, finely chopped

4 shallots, thinly sliced

Cronch Topping (page 75), for serving

1. Using a mandoline, sharp vegetable peeler, or chef's knife, prep the daikon and pears. Roughly crush the grapes by hand.

2. In a large bowl, lightly toss the radicchio leaves with the miso citrus dressing, a hefty drizzle of olive oil, and the lemon juice. Add the daikon, pears, grapes, chives, and shallots. Toss again until everything is covered in dressing.

3. Plate the dressed salad and sprinkle with cronch topping to serve.

Shiso Onigiri

Serves 6

Onigiri is my favorite way to serve rice when I am having people over. I wouldn't normally go through the process of shaping these beautiful, structured triangles just for myself, so it makes having rice on the table feel all the more special. I like to add edible flowers and furikake to the rice and wrap it with shiso leaves instead of the traditional seaweed, although seaweed is a wonderful substitute if you're looking for one. While the onigiri are great on their own, I like having 2 to 3 onigiri per person on my vegetable-and-fish-filled table to add a bright, starchy balance and give people something to munch on between building their lettuce cups. I recommend you dip your onigiri in The Best Green Sauce (page 77) or the Universal Dipping Sauce (page 76).

4 to 6 cups freshly cooked sushi rice (see Note)
Sea salt
2 tablespoons rice vinegar
2 teaspoons toasted sesame oil
Furikake and/or dried edible flowers
6 to 8 shiso leaves

Note: About ⅓ cup of uncooked rice makes one onigiri, so budget how much rice you cook according to your guest count. Cook the rice according to the package directions.

1. Once the rice is fluffy and cooked through, add a pinch of salt, the rice vinegar, and sesame oil. Taste and adjust. Let cool and fold in either furikake, dried edible flowers, or both!

2. Prepare a small bowl with water next to your workstation. With wet hands, take ¾ cup of rice and shape it into a triangle. It may feel loose to start, but as the water evaporates, the rice will stick together more and more. The shiso leaves are acting as the seaweed, so make sure they are big enough so the triangle is in the center of the shiso. Wrap the leaf at the base on the onigiri, letting it wrap and fold around the sides, or simply lay the rice triangle on a leaf for presentation's sake.

Beautifully constructed onigiri are always a delight for guests, and they make the table that much more interesting. While there are lots of ways to accomplish the onigiri fold, here's my tried-and-true method for getting consistent, pretty onigiri prepped and ready.

STEP ONE
Dampen your hands with a bit of salty water. Scoop about ¾ cup of rice and start to mold the rice into a triangular shape by cupping your fingers into a C-shape, while packing the rice down.

STEP TWO
Place the rice at the end of the bottom of the shiso leaf, making sure the tip of the triangle is pointing toward the tip of the leaf.

STEP THREE
Fold the top and bottom of the leaf onto the rice. The stickiness of the rice should help keep it in place.

STEP FOUR
Decorate with more furikake and edible flowers.

Fish Three Ways

I associate fish with abundance, and I don't think I am the only one. Why else would we choose fish, of all things, in the age-old *teach a man to fish* proverb? In this way, serving fish feels right for the promise of spring. What follows are three different preparation and cooking styles to choose from for your fish dish. Consider it a "choose your own adventure" where you pick one fish to anchor your table. The fried fish is inspired by my Ma. It's the dish she would welcome me home with and the recipe that reminds me most of my origins. The salmon is zippy and bright, making good use of the season's herbs. If you have a particularly herbaceous haul at the farmers' market, maybe this is the fish dish for you. And finally, the stuffed fish is on a whole other level. It's heartier and individually plated because everyone gets their own fish (fun). If you envision more sitting and less grazing, this is the fish for you.

Ma's Fried Fish

Serves 6

This recipe is inspired by the way my grandma prepares the moon fish that my grandpa catches. It's the kind of dish she would pull together if she knew you were coming over—and one I've enjoyed some version of most of my life. Needless to say, it's dear to my heart and also super easy to make. It's not uncommon for me to have it at least once or twice a week with the Universal Dipping Sauce (page 76). This is one I would definitely recommend you eat with your hands, building little bites with lettuces and toppings.

Vegetable oil, for shallow-frying

2 cups all-purpose flour

Fine sea salt

Eight 3- to 4-ounce sockeye salmon fillets

1. Pour ⅓ inch of vegetable oil into a cast-iron pan and bring the oil to 350°F over medium heat.

2. Meanwhile, in a bowl, mix the flour and 1 tablespoon salt. Salt both sides of the fish and lightly coat with the flour mixture by patting it in with your hands. The fish should be coated on both sides evenly, but not thickly.

3. Drop the fish skin side down into the oil. It should immediately start to sizzle, but not violently. Cook until the skin self-releases from the pan, 5 to 7 minutes. Carefully flip and cook until the fish is deep and golden in color and juicy on the inside, about an additional 5 minutes.

4. Slice the fish into about 2-inch pieces, then assemble on a serving plate.

Ping Pa (Stuffed Trout)

Serves 6

I love a stuffed fish. The eating experience brings me back to something primal and communal. It's sort of an unspoken rule to eat it in a group setting, passing it around and eating every last bite until all that's left is bone. This aromatic fish is delightful with the accoutrement board and dipping sauces. This dish is usually made with red snapper, but if this is your first time hosting a dinner party, using trout will be easier to plan because of their size. They're typically 1 to 2 pounds, making them perfectly personal-size. I definitely invite you to try a bigger fish when you're ready. Just be sure to watch out for small bones!

6 whole trout (about 1 pound each), cleaned, scaled, and boned

Fine sea salt

Olive oil, for drizzling

1 cup Miso Citrus Dressing (page 76)

4 lemons, sliced into rounds

6 medium shallots, halved lengthwise and thinly sliced

2 thumbs ginger, peeled and sliced

Cloves from 2 heads garlic, sliced

4 stalks lemongrass, thinly sliced

18 makrut lime leaves (optional)

1 bunch of Thai basil, roughly torn

1 bunch of cilantro, roughly torn

1. Line a sheet pan with parchment paper. Pat the fish dry and lay on the lined pan. Lightly salt the inside and both sides of each fish, then drizzle with olive oil and brush on the miso citrus dressing. Lightly brush the dressing on the inside of the fish, too. Line one side of flesh with 3 to 4 lemon slices. Stuff each fish with the equal amounts of shallots, ginger, garlic, and lemongrass. If using makrut lime leaves, add 3 to each fish. Wrap the whole pan with plastic wrap and let sit for at least 3 hours in the fridge, and up to overnight.

2. Preheat the oven to 375°F.

3. Uncover the fish and bake until the fish is fully cooked and fragrant, 10 to 15 minutes.

4. Sprinkle generously with the basil and cilantro and serve.

Herby Olive Grilled Salmon

Serves 6

I made this on a whim a few summers ago and wow, was it good. The fat from the fish balances perfectly with the briny, brightness from the lemon and olives. This one will become one of your grilling favorites. If you don't have access to an outdoor grill, you can also use a ridged cast-iron grill pan inside.

Six ½-pound skin-on sockeye salmon fillets

3 cups The Best Green Sauce (page 77), plus more for serving

Olive oil, for drizzling

Lemon wedges, for squeezing

1. Line a large bowl with a sealable bag. Pat the fish dry. Add the fish and sauce to the sealable bag and mix until the fillets are fully coated. Seal the bag so that it's airtight and let marinate for at least 1 to 2 hours and up to overnight in the fridge.

2. Clean the grates of your grill and oil the grates with an oiled paper towel. Bring the grill to medium heat.

3. Add the salmon to the grill skin side down over direct heat (over the flame). Cover the grill and cook until the skin is browned and releases easily from the grates, 5 to 8 minutes. Carefully flip the fish and let it cook until the fish is completely cooked through to your preferred temperature, about another 5 minutes. I like medium, about 140°F. (Alternatively, to cook on a cast-iron grill pan, oil the pan well and cook the salmon over medium heat until the skin self-releases. Then flip and continue to cook until you've reached your desired temperature.)

4. Slice the salmon into 2-inch pieces, then brush with more fresh Best Green Sauce, a drizzle of olive oil, and a squeeze of lemon. If you have leftover herbs—you will—use them to decorate your platter as a final touch.

Pandan & Coconut Jellies with Fruit

Serves 2

Your bellies are full; everyone is enjoying themselves and have made new friends! What better way to end the evening than with some lightly sweetened jelly with fresh spring fruits? Sometimes I crave something sweet after a meal to balance the palate, but don't want anything too heavy or else I'll pop. This is the perfect medium. It's tasty, light, and when served with fruits, the most satisfying way to end a meal. The pandan gives the jelly a vibrant (and totally natural) green hue and earthy, sweet flavor. You can usually find its extract at your local Asian market or online. If you're having dinner outside, I would recommend making this ahead of time and pulling it out of the fridge right before you're about to serve.

Pandan Jelly

1 can (400ml) pandan leaf extract (note: not the concentrate!)

90 grams (about ½ cup) sugar

10 grams (about 2 tablespoons) agar-agar

¼ teaspoon fine sea salt

Coconut Jelly

1½ cans (400ml each) unsweetened coconut milk

90 grams (about ½ cup) sugar

10 grams (about 2 tablespoons) agar-agar

¼ teaspoon fine sea salt

For Serving

Fruits, like mango, lychee, dragon fruit, melon, passion fruit, and strawberries

1. Make the pandan jelly: In a medium pot, combine the pandan leaf extract, sugar, agar-agar, salt, and ¾ cup plus 1½ tablespoons (200g) of water. Set over medium heat and bring to a simmer, whisking, until the sugar is dissolved, 3 to 5 minutes. Remove from the heat.

2. Make the coconut jelly: In a separate medium pot, combine the coconut milk, sugar, agar-agar, and salt. Set over medium heat and bring to a simmer, whisking, until the sugar is dissolved. Remove from the heat.

3. Using a bowl or mold that can hold at least 6 cups, build your pandan and coconut layers. You can easily just do two layers (coconut on the bottom, pandan on the top) or you can pour ¾ cup at a time to create a striped mold. Whatever style you choose, pour one layer in liquid form into the mold and allow the layer to fully set before pouring in another. When the pandan layer is firm to the touch but still slightly warm (the agar-agar sets at room temperature), gently pour the coconut layer on top. You can use a toothpick to pop any bubbles.

4. Cover the mold with plastic wrap and refrigerate for about 4 hours. Serve with cut fruits, like mango, lychee, dragon fruit, melon, passion fruit, and strawberries.

Eat Everything

My philosophy on plating is as follows: If it's on a plate, you should be able to eat it. Nothing honors nature and all her bounty more than an abundant plate where everything accompanying the dish can be experienced, enjoyed. I love to cram my plates with tons of herbs, leaves, and edible flowers, which in turn encourages play and interaction with the dish. It invites curiosity and a sense of adventure. Will that leaf be bitter or sweet? What will that flower taste like? Is it as crunchy as it looks or will it melt in my mouth? No two bites are the same. Everyone's experiences are unique. Freshness takes center stage and makes us feel close to the earth. Plus, it's a great way to make sure you get through all the bounty you picked up at the market. Have leftover shiso leaves? Dry them out and make a yummy shiso salt. Give cilantro an entirely new context. Play with broccoli flowers (which, in case you've never tried, taste exactly like broccoli!). Find some arugula that was so happy in the ground it sprouted little yellow flowers. The result, I promise, is both delicious and beautiful.

6 DAYS OUT

Confirm how many guests you have and if they have any allergies or dietary preferences.

Do you have everything you need in the table setting department? Enough glassware, silverware, serving spoons?

Decide how big you want to go with the tablescape. Are you printing menu cards? Simple flower arrangements?

5 DAYS OUT

Write a menu and all ingredients needed for each dish. Write where you can source your ingredients. Clean out the fridge and make space.

2 DAYS OUT

Double check if all guests are still confirmed. Perhaps send a text saying that you're excited for their company and looking forward to seeing them soon.

I suggest tidying up your kitchen and dining area. I know you'll probably get your kitchen somewhat dirty again with prep, but for me it's essential to work with a clean space. Helps the flow leading up to the event.

1 DAY OUT

I personally like to do groceries the day before to ensure freshness, especially when it comes to produce. I would go early in the morning so you can be back by the afternoon to start prep.

Make any sauces, marinate fish if necessary, and clean all produce and properly store with paper towels in airtight containers.

If you decided to do a simple flower arrangement, I would pick up the flowers on this day and process them by cutting the stems at an angle, trimming excess leaves, and storing them in water at room temperature.

Prepare the Pandan & Coconut Jellies and store in the refrigerator.

DINNER PARTY!

Clean all dishes, serving ware, glasses, and silverware in the morning and set aside.

Prepare all vegetables, herbs, and fish dish of choice.

Batch any drinks if necessary.

Put the final touches on the tablescape.

Serve up your dishes and enjoy your company for the evening!

First of the Season BBQ

WITH BILL CLARK

Bill is a writer, recipe developer, and chef. You may know him from the beloved Brooklyn establishment MeMe's Diner or from his viral recipes like pizza babka. In his personal time, Bill is an extraordinarily welcoming host with a "the more the merrier" approach to bringing people together.

MAY

STEAL MY PLAYLIST

About eight years ago, I found myself in one of the worst places a New Yorker can find themselves: I needed to secure a new apartment in, like, the next week. I began an appropriately panicked search, viewing any and every living space available.

With four days to spare, I stumbled across a Craigslist ad for a basement apartment on the edge of Clinton Hill and Bed-Stuy in Brooklyn. When I went to see the place an hour later, I was met with a nice surprise: a large backyard with a big square concrete patio. It was disused, muddy, and a little bleak, but it was there. I started writing the deposit check before the landlord had even confirmed it was private to the apartment. (It was.) I didn't know it at the time, but having a backyard changed the trajectory of my life in Brooklyn and turned me into a near-expert outdoor entertainer.

After eight summers, a fence, some paint, an old, salvaged sink, and one *giant* grapevine, our backyard has become my social life's three-season center of gravity. That is to say, I've thrown some great parties back here. I'm talking midnight grilled lobsters and champagne; a last-minute twenty-person seated dinner; and a Big Gay Backyard Disco Party the summer I met my now-husband. There have been countless post–Riis Beach grilled dinners and Friday happy-hours-turned-dinner-turned-late-night parties. Through all this partying, there have been many lessons that I have learned (or ignored)—too many to share here. But one in particular has shaped the way I host and inspired this particular gathering . . .

If you only take one thing away from this chapter, let it be the greatest lesson I've learned in all my years of backyard entertaining: Always host the first party of any season. I can't take full credit for this brilliant strategy—it's actually a bit of party advice I picked up from my mother, who always hosted the first Christmas party of the year. Whether it's the winter holidays or the start of summer, being the first one on the

books means everyone will be thrilled to be at your party, and you get to set the tone for the season. Even if you schedule yours just ahead of the actual season, being the primary party is still a power move. By your friend group's fourth holiday cocktail party or the fifth BBQ of Memorial Day weekend, enthusiasm will have waned and they'll be comparing those later parties to yours. Securing your spot as "First of the Season" party requires a longer lead time, so don't shy away from appearing a little eager. If anything, time is on your side this way—you get to capture everyone's summer excitement and get maximum festive spirit by getting your invites out early.

You don't have to live in New York City to understand how glorious outdoor living spaces are, but seeing as they are extra rare here, you can understand how exciting it is when the weather is warm enough and I finally get the chance to host outdoors. Nothing signals the end of winter like the ritual of waking the backyard from its dormant state, cleaning up the patio, and preparing the first guest list of the season. For this reason alone, my inaugural Memorial Day BBQ is one of my favorite parties of the year.

If you're going to claim the title "First of the Season" party, there are four key components you must include in your start-of-summer BBQ: a strong beverage plan, at least two protein and vegetable options, sides that aren't an afterthought, and a crowd-pleaser of a dessert. Extra points (always) for snacks. The menu presented in the chapter finds a nice balance between classic and unexpected BBQ favorites, and is sure to please even the pickiest eaters. Now, go refill that propane tank.

Pack a Punch: Three Variations on the Perfect Party Punch

I tend to shy away from "one and ones," a booze and a mixer, for outdoor daytime parties. It's too easy for folks to make themselves a stiff one and it's too much fuss around the bar. Instead, I shoot for a prebatched punch that I make ahead of time and pour into swing-top bottles.

A perfect punch has three main components: the spirit, the acid, and the sweet. The choices of booze and vehicles for the flavors are essentially endless, but keep balance in mind if you're building your own. All of these recipes are designed to make about 2 quarts and can be scaled up or down to accommodate your guest count. To scale down for single-serving drinks, for example, simply replace cup measurements with ounces. Each of these recipes is prepared by simply combining the ingredients and decanting into a vessel of choice. Serve chilled.

The Odder Cape Codder

Serves 8

Name a more classic and simpler cocktail than a vodka cranberry. This Cape Cod variation pumps up the flavor and makes it less boozy (with less vodka), taking a note from its cousin, the Seabreeze.

¼ cup grapefruit juice

¼ cup dry vermouth

¾ cup simple syrup

¾ cup fresh lime juice

1 cup sparkling wine or seltzer

2 cups vodka

3 cups unsweetened cranberry juice

Combine the ingredients and decant into a vessel of choice. Chill well before serving.

The Dark Daiq

Serves 8

This is the classic daiquiri's more sophisticated cousin, who happens to be an excellent party guest.

¼ cup allspice dram
¾ cup fresh lime juice
¾ cup simple syrup
1 cup white rum
1 cup dark rum
1 cup sparkling wine or seltzer
3 cups strong black tea

Combine the ingredients and decant into a vessel of choice. Chill well before serving.

Spritz'groni

Serves 8

Not quite an Aperol spritz but not quite a Negroni. Something a little less sweet with a hint of bitter. Great with tangy BBQ.

½ cup sweet vermouth
½ cup orange juice
1 cup Aperol
1 cup Campari
1 cup gin
4 cups sparkling wine

Combine the ingredients and decant into a vessel of choice. Chill well before serving.

What Goes on the Grill

One grilled entree is dinner, but three grilled options are a party—especially when each comes with an accompanying sauce. With some planning ahead, you can serve all three at the same time, ensuring something for every guest without breaking a sweat.

New York Vinegary Marinade & Chicken

Makes enough marinade for 6 pounds of chicken

I say this with every confidence: This is the most useful marinade you'll ever make, hailing straight from my childhood in western New York. While the southern states might be world-famous for their regional barbecue styles, western New York's BBQ chicken deserves a seat at the table. All summer long, in school parking lots and on the side of country highways, big trailer-style charcoal grills are cooking hundreds of half chickens soaked in this vinegary marinade. My version of the marinade is a little more downstate, but the tenderizing punch of vinegar is still at the heart of it. Scale this recipe up for bigger parties; it's easily doubled.

New York Vinegary Marinade

2 cups apple cider vinegar

1 egg

2 tablespoons kosher salt

½ teaspoon freshly ground black pepper

½ teaspoon Aleppo pepper

1 tablespoon Dijon mustard

1 tablespoon poultry seasoning

1 cup neutral oil, such as canola or peanut

6 pounds chicken (I prefer thighs and legs, but half chickens or bone-in breasts work, too)

Garden Green Sauce (page 102), for serving

1. Make the marinade: Combine all the marinade ingredients but the oil in a blender, then pulse until combined. With the blender still running, stream in the oil to emulsify.

2. Divide the chicken into two 1-gallon zip-seal bags. Pour half of the marinade into each bag. Press the air out of each and marinate in the fridge for at least 3 hours and up to 6. Marinate overnight for the best flavor.

3. Preheat a grill to medium hot. Grill the chicken, turning occasionally, until the internal temperature reaches 165°F close to the bone, around 20 minutes.

4. Serve with garden green sauce.

Make Ahead: You can store the marinade in an airtight container in the refrigerator for up to 1 week.

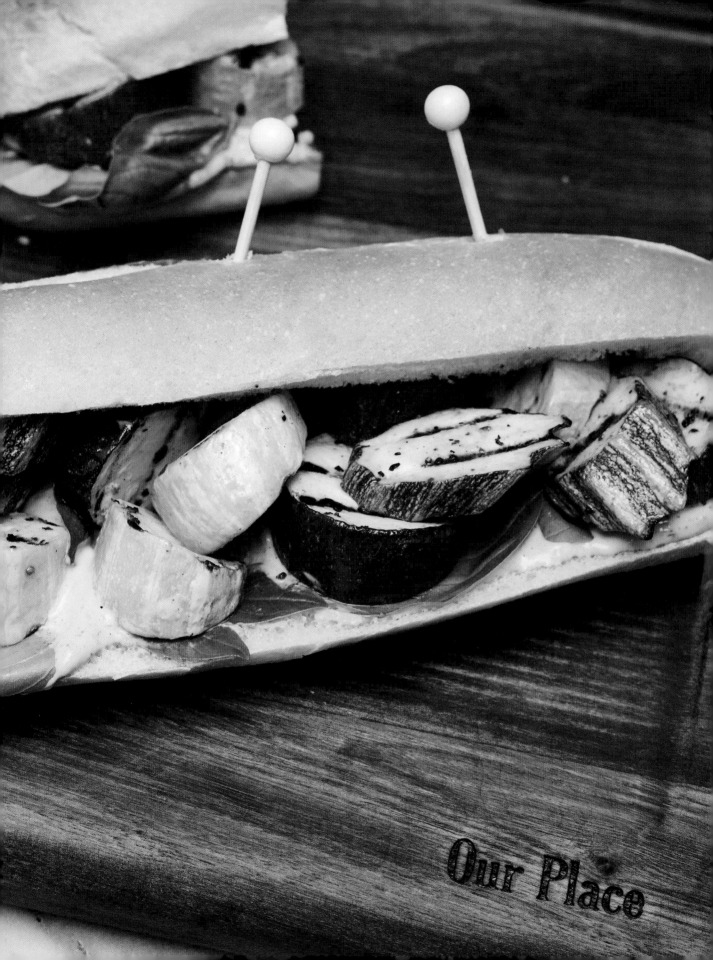

Our Place

Zucchini Spiedies

Makes 12 sandwiches

Spiedies (pronounced "speedys") is another regional favorite of mine. A traditional spiedie is chicken breast or lamb with a vinegary-style marinade, cooked on skewers and served on an Italian-style hoagie roll. This zucchini variation is a veggie sandwich that omnivores will crave, too. I just can't help myself.

The trick to a great grilled zucchini sandwich is the cut of the veggie. I cut my zukes into oblique chunks, instead of discs or strips. When you grill them, the thinner side gets nice and soft while the thicker side keeps some bite and heft. The combo of textures, plus the sandwich sauce, really makes this sandwich.

6 pounds zucchini
New York Vinegary Marinade (page 97)
Salt
Apple cider vinegar
Four 10- to 12-inch Italian-style hoagie rolls
Sandwich Sauce (page 102)
Handful of fresh basil leaves

1. Cut the zucchini into oblique chunks, about 1 inch on the thick side tapering to about ¼ inch. To achieve the right shape, I rotate the zucchini between cuts. Divide the zucchini into two 1-gallon zip-seal bags. Divide the marinade evenly between the two. Press the air out of each and marinate in the fridge for at least 3 hours and up to 6.

2. Preheat the grill to medium. Grill the zucchini chunks directly on the grates, turning occasionally, until they have a nice char. Test one. It should be soft but still have some bite after about 10 minutes. Remove to a tray and season with salt and a splash of apple cider vinegar to taste.

3. Slice the hoagie rolls lengthwise but not all the way through. Spread open and scrape out about half the interior bread on each side. This makes the perfect bread-to-veggie ratio. Spread generously with sandwich sauce and line with the fresh basil leaves.

4. Evenly divide the grilled zucchini among the rolls. Close the sandwich and secure with three sandwich picks for each roll. Cut each into 3 pieces, creating twelve 3- to 4-inch sandwiches.

Twice-Cooked Ribs

Serves 6 to 8

There seems to be some kind of shared belief that making ribs has to be very difficult. Every time I bust out this rib recipe at a party, everyone gets excited: "Wow, I can't believe you made ribs!" My rib recipe is prep-heavy, but pretty easy, making it the perfect do-ahead recipe that you simply finish on the grill (. . . but you don't have to tell your guests that). They're best done a day ahead and allowed to chill overnight in the fridge. This makes them super easy to handle the next day and they come to temp on the grill in about 15 minutes or less.

About 6 pounds pork spareribs

2 tablespoons paprika

1 tablespoon ground ginger

1 tablespoon Aleppo pepper

1 teaspoon ground coriander

¼ cup Dijon mustard

2 tablespoons kosher salt

2 tablespoons apple cider vinegar

1 small orange, quartered, peel
  and all

¼ cup honey

1 can light beer, like a pilsner

Burnt Honey BBQ (page 103)

1. Remove the silver skin from the bone side of the ribs—you can work your finger under and remove in strips. This step is not completely necessary, but makes for a nicer end product. There is a thicker end of the rack and a thinner end of the rack. Divide the racks at the rib where they start to get noticeably thinner. This will allow them to fit on a sheet pan and also give you more control with the final grill (the thinner end will, of course, cook faster). Place them on a foil-lined sheet pan; overlapping is fine.

2. In a high-powered blender or food processor, combine the paprika, ground ginger, Aleppo, coriander, mustard, salt, vinegar, orange pieces, and honey. Pulse to combine. Add splashes of beer until it all comes together into a loose paste. Slather all sides of the ribs with the marinade paste. Cover and refrigerate for at least 4 hours or overnight. If necessary, you can skip the resting period, but the flavor is better with a longer marination.

3. Preheat the oven to 325°F.

4. Remove the ribs from the fridge. Uncover and pour ½ cup of the remaining beer into the bottom of the sheet pan. Cover very tightly with foil.

5. Roast until the meat is fork-tender and beginning to fall off the bone but while the racks still stay together, 2½ to 3 hours.

6. Remove from the oven, leaving it on the pan, and cool to room temperature before transferring to the refrigerator. Chill until cold, preferably overnight.

7. Preheat the grill to medium-high. Place the cold ribs on the grill. Baste with burnt honey BBQ, turning and basting until the ribs are heated through and have developed a nice glaze with a bit of char.

8. Slice into 3-rib chunks and serve with the remaining BBQ sauce on the side.

Garden Green Sauce

Makes 3 cups

A fresh all-purpose sauce that brightens up grilled chicken but is equally good with grilled steak or pork chops.

1 small shallot, finely minced

½ serrano pepper, finely minced, with seeds

¼ cup fresh lemon juice

1 cup packed fresh cilantro leaves, finely chopped

1 cup packed fresh parsley leaves, finely chopped

1 cup packed fresh mint leaves, finely chopped

½ cup packed fresh basil leaves, finely chopped

1 cup olive oil

1 teaspoon honey

1 teaspoon salt

¼ teaspoon freshly ground black pepper

In a medium bowl, combine the shallot, serrano, and lemon juice. Add the cilantro, parsley, mint, and basil. Stir in the olive oil and honey. Season with the salt and black pepper. Let the flavors rest to come together. It's best after storing overnight in the refrigerator and keeps in an airtight container for up to 1 week.

Sandwich Sauce

Makes 4 cups

A flavor bomb for all sandwiches, but especially the Zucchini Spiedies (page 99). It's spicy, tangy, and just mellow enough for it to be great on bread.

4 ounces drained jarred Peppadew peppers

2-inch knob fresh ginger, peeled

2 tablespoons rice vinegar

1 tablespoon gochujang (Korean chile paste)

2 cups mayonnaise

1 cup sour cream

2 tablespoons Dijon mustard

1 teaspoon Worcestershire sauce

½ teaspoon freshly ground black pepper

½ teaspoon salt

¼ teaspoon MSG

In a food processor, finely chop the drained peppers. Pour off any liquid that remains after chopping. Add the ginger, vinegar, and gochujang and process until finely chopped. Add the mayo, sour cream, mustard, Worcestershire sauce, black pepper, salt, and MSG. Pulse until just combined. Transfer to an airtight container and refrigerate for up to 2 weeks.

Burnt Honey BBQ

Serves 6 to 8

Super tangy, slightly spicy, and a subtle bitter bite. This sauce definitely benefits from an overnight rest in the fridge, so it's great to make this ahead of time!

¾ cup honey

One 12-ounce can light beer, like a pilsner

One 6-ounce can tomato paste

2 teaspoons garlic powder

1 teaspoon onion powder

½ teaspoon ground allspice

½ teaspoon ground ginger

½ teaspoon freshly ground black pepper

½ teaspoon Aleppo pepper

1½ teaspoons salt

2 tablespoons apple cider vinegar

1. In a medium saucepan, bring the honey to a boil over medium-high heat and whisk occasionally to keep from boiling over. Cook until the honey is visibly darkened and smells slightly burnt, 8 to 12 minutes depending on the honey. Remove from the heat and carefully pour in the can of beer while whisking. Be careful of the steam.

2. Return to medium heat and whisk in the tomato paste, garlic powder, onion powder, allspice, ginger, black pepper, Aleppo, salt, and vinegar. Cook at a steady simmer until thickened to desired consistency. I like a sauce on the thinner side. This can be made well ahead of time and stored in an airtight container in the refrigerator.

All Green Slaw

Serves 6 to 8

This late-spring slaw is all green, but far from boring. With hearty napa cabbage as the base, the other textures (ribboned and sliced asparagus, whole snow peas, and slivered snap peas) can shine. Tying it all together is a fresh, slightly funky blue cheese green goddess dressing. Keep this dressing recipe in your back pocket: It's great on a sandwich, as a dipping sauce, or on any other salad.

Blue Cheese Green Goddess Dressing

1 cup packed fresh cilantro

1 cup packed fresh basil

1 cup packed fresh mint

1 garlic clove

1 tablespoon fresh lemon juice

1 cup whole-milk Greek yogurt

¾ cup mayonnaise

2 tablespoons Dijon mustard

¼ pound blue cheese, crumbled

½ teaspoon Worcestershire sauce

½ teaspoon salt, plus more to taste

½ teaspoon freshly ground black pepper

½ teaspoon honey

Slaw

1 small head napa cabbage

½ pound snap peas

1 pound snow peas

2 bunches of asparagus

Salt, to taste

Fresh lemon juice, to taste

3 scallions, thinly sliced on the diagonal

Blue cheese crumbles, for garnish

1. Make the blue cheese green goddess dressing: In a food processor, combine the cilantro, basil, mint, garlic, and lemon juice. Pulse until chopped (it does not need to be finely chopped yet).

2. Add the yogurt, mayo, mustard, blue cheese, Worcestershire sauce, salt, pepper, and honey. Run the food processor until the mixture is almost smooth. Some remaining texture from the cheese is a good thing. Taste for salt, depending on your cheese. Refrigerate in an airtight container for up to 1 week.

3. Make the slaw: Slice the cabbage into ¼-inch ribbons. Thinly slice the snap peas on the diagonal. Roughly cut the snow peas in half. Place in a large bowl.

4. Snap off the tough ends of the asparagus. Using a Y-peeler, holding on to the spear of the asparagus, run the peeler the length of the asparagus, making very thin ribbons. Trim the spears off and slice them in half lengthwise. Add the ribbons and the halved spears to the bowl.

5. Toss the slaw with a generous amount of dressing. You want it to be fully dressed but not heavy and soggy. Season with salt and lemon juice to taste. Transfer to a serving bowl. Garnish with the scallions and some blue cheese.

Salt Potato Salad with Drawn Butter Vinaigrette

Serves 10 to 12

In case you're not familiar, let me introduce you to another staple of my homeland of Upstate New York: the salt potato. Like a really salty potato. I want to see a white skim coat of salt on each tiny boiled potato. I originally intended this potato salad to be an ode to that glorious side dish of my youth, but the tangy butter vinaigrette ended up evoking memories of a lobster boil on Cape Cod. I'm not mad at that either. Truly, if a New England boil were a salad, it would be this. You can easily halve this recipe, including the salt for the boiling water.

Salt Potatoes

6 pounds baby red potatoes, the smallest you can find, rinsed

2 cups salt

Vinaigrette

1 cup ghee or clarified butter

⅓ cup apple cider vinegar

2 tablespoons fresh lemon juice

1 tablespoon Dijon mustard

One 2-inch chunk of the white part of a scallion

For Serving

Loosely chopped fresh dill

Grated lemon zest

1. Make the salt potatoes: Place the baby potatoes in an 8-quart pot and cover with cold water. Add the salt; no need to stir. Bring to a boil and cook until fork-tender but not too soft. Drain and set aside. They're best at room temperature and not refrigerated.

2. Make the vinaigrette: In a small pan, melt the ghee. Set aside to cool slightly.

3. In a blender, combine the vinegar, lemon juice, mustard, and scallion. Process until smooth. With the blender running, stream in the melted ghee. Store in an airtight container at room temperature to prevent the ghee from solidifying for up to 2 days or in the refrigerator for up to 2 weeks. If you are making it ahead of time, keep it refrigerated; just warm it slightly and re-emulsify before using.

4. In a bowl, toss the room temperature or slightly warm salt potatoes in a generous amount of the vinaigrette. Garnish with a lot of dill and lemon zest.

Root Beer Baked Beans

Serves 6 to 8

Yes, baked beans are already sweet, sometimes cloyingly so. But what if all that brown sugar and molasses was replaced with root beer? I'll tell you: It's delicious. Use the nicest root beer you can find—it will make a difference. Your guests might not be able to put their finger on exactly what that subtle flavor is in the beans, but they'll love it.

2 pounds dried Great Northern beans

Five 12-ounce bottles root beer

2 medium yellow onions

2 bay leaves

2 guajillo chiles

½ small navel orange

2 whole star anise

2 tablespoons kosher salt, plus more to taste

2 tablespoons olive oil

4 garlic cloves, thinly sliced

¼ teaspoon Aleppo pepper

½ teaspoon freshly ground black pepper, plus more to taste

¼ teaspoon ground cinnamon

One 6-ounce can tomato paste

2 tablespoons hoisin sauce

1 tablespoon apple cider vinegar, plus more to taste

Salt

1. Rinse the beans well. Drain and place them in a 5- to 6-quart Dutch oven with 4 bottles of the root beer and 1 cup cold water. Soak overnight.

2. Place the beans in their soaking liquid over medium-low heat. Add water if the beans are not covered by liquid. Peel and quarter 1 onion and add it to the beans along with the bay leaves, dried chiles, orange, star anise, and salt. Simmer until the beans are completely tender but not soft and the skins are intact, 30 to 45 minutes. Remove from the heat and discard the aromatics. Transfer the beans to a bowl.

3. Preheat the oven to 325°F.

4. Finely chop the second onion. In the Dutch oven, heat the olive oil over medium-low heat. Add the onion and garlic and cook until translucent, 5 to 6 minutes. Add the Aleppo pepper, black pepper, and cinnamon and cook until fragrant.

5. Add the tomato paste and hoisin sauce and cook until the mixture is caramelized and begins to stick to the bottom of the pot. Deglaze with the remaining 1 bottle root beer. Stir in the vinegar and cooked beans. Bring to a simmer and taste for salt, black pepper, and vinegar. Adjust to taste.

6. Transfer to the oven and bake until the beans and sauce are to your desired consistency, 1 to 1½ hours. I took mine to 1½ hours, but for a saucier bean, bake less. Serve warm.

Strawberry Cream Cheese Slab Pie

Serves 25

I can't remember the first time I made a slab pie for a crowd, but it was a milestone in my life. Honestly, it's not much more work than making a standard 9-inch pie, but this one feeds a crowd and looks like a star. It shows off the berries that are just coming into season in the Northeast, ribboned into a base of sweet cream cheese in a buttery crust. This crust recipe is another to hang on to—it can be used for a slab pie in any season. You can cut this recipe in half and bake it on a quarter-sheet pan instead.

Crust

4 cups all-purpose flour

2 tablespoons sugar

2 teaspoons kosher salt

1 pound unsalted butter, cubed and frozen

1 cup cold water

Jam

2 pounds strawberries

½ cup sugar

Juice of 1 lemon

½ teaspoon kosher salt

2 tablespoons cornstarch

Cream Cheese Filling

1½ pounds cream cheese, at room temperature

¾ cup sugar

2 large eggs

Grated zest of 1 lemon

½ teaspoon kosher salt

3 tablespoons all-purpose flour

Assembly

Egg wash; 1 egg, well whisked

Raw sugar, for sprinkling

(continued)

1. Make the crust: Working in two batches in a food processor, add 2 cups flour, 1 tablespoon sugar, and 1 teaspoon salt and pulse to combine. Add half of the butter to the food processor. Pulse until the mixture resembles coarse meal and there are pea-size pieces of butter remaining. Transfer the mixture to a large bowl and repeat the process with the second half.

2. Drizzle the cold water a couple tablespoons at a time over the butter-flour mixture. Using your fingertips, incorporate the water, being careful to not overwork or knead, until the dough sticks together but is not sticky. Gently press into a disc and wrap tightly with plastic. Refrigerate for at least 1 hour and up to overnight. Keep refrigerated until ready to use.

3. Make the jam: Hull and slice the strawberries into a medium saucepan. Add the sugar, lemon juice, and salt. Cook over medium heat until the strawberries begin to soften and their juices are released, about 8 minutes.

4. Ladle out about ¼ cup of the strawberry juice into a small bowl. Whisk in the cornstarch until completely combined and smooth. Return to the saucepan and continue to cook until the mixture comes to a boil and is thickened. Spread on a sheet pan and cool in the refrigerator.

5. Make the cream cheese filling: In a food processor, combine the cream cheese, sugar, eggs, lemon zest, salt, and flour. Set aside until ready to use.

6. Preheat the oven to 425°F.

7. Assemble the pie: Divide off two-thirds of the dough. On a well-floured surface, roll into a rectangle 15½ × 20½ inches. Line a half-sheet pan with the dough; it should come up the sides with a ¼-inch overlap. Pro tip: You can roll the dough out on the silicone Oven Mat and make the transfer to the pan extra easy.

8. Spread the cream cheese filling evenly over the pie shell. Place the sheet pan in the fridge while you prepare the remaining crust.

9. Roll the remaining one-third of the dough into a rectangle roughly 9 × 20 inches. Using a roller cutter, slice the dough lengthwise into strips 1½ inches wide and 20 inches long.

10. Remove the filled crust from the refrigerator and dot the cream cheese with the strawberry jam. The jam should be evenly distributed, but some patches of cream cheese should show.

11. Lay the pie crust strips across the pie on top of the jam on a diagonal. You may basket weave them if desired. Finish by tucking in the ¼-inch overhang in the ends of the strips. Brush the crust with the egg wash and sprinkle with raw sugar.

12. Transfer the pie to the floor of the oven (or the very lowest rack) and bake for 10 minutes. Move to a rack in the center of the oven and bake until the crust is golden and crisp, another 35 to 40 minutes.

13. Let cool completely. Slice the pie in a 5-by-5 grid to create 25 servings.

Make Ahead: Store the cake in the refrigerator tightly wrapped in plastic for up to 1 week. Before serving, either bring it to room temperature on the counter or place it in a warm oven for a couple of minutes.

Chile Chocolate Sheet Cake

Serves 25

No joke, it's kind of a given that cake will be served at nearly all functions in my home. This recipe is super easy and one to refer to and tinker with flavors on your own. I love the texture that comes out when the glaze is poured on the cake while still hot. Deeply toasted pecans, chipotle chile, and cinnamon make this one special. You could try it with another nut, swap in espresso powder for the chile, or try any other of the endless variations. But give this one a go first. You can cut this recipe in half and bake it on a quarter-sheet pan instead.

Sheet Cake

Nonstick cooking spray

2 cups all-purpose flour

4 tablespoons unsweetened cocoa powder

1 teaspoon baking soda

2 cups granulated sugar

2 teaspoons kosher salt

½ cup buttermilk

2 eggs

1 teaspoon vanilla extract

2 sticks (8 ounces) unsalted butter, melted

1 cup very hot water

Glaze

14 tablespoons (7 ounces) unsalted butter

¼ cup unsweetened cocoa powder

½ teaspoon ground cinnamon

½ teaspoon chipotle chile powder

½ teaspoon kosher salt

6 tablespoons whole milk

1 pound minus ½ cup powdered sugar, sifted

1 teaspoon vanilla extract

1 cup pecans, deeply toasted and finely chopped

1. Make the sheet cake: Preheat the oven to 350°F. Spray a half-sheet pan with cooking spray.

2. In a large bowl, sift together the flour, cocoa powder, and baking soda. Whisk in the sugar and salt. In a separate small bowl or measuring cup, whisk together the buttermilk, eggs, and vanilla. Add to the dry ingredients along with the melted butter. Whisk to combine. Add the very hot water and whisk until a loose batter forms. Scrape down the sides and bottom of the bowl to ensure everything is combined. Spread the batter evenly in the sheet pan.

3. Bake until the center of the cake springs back slightly when touched, about 20 minutes.

4. Meanwhile, make the glaze: In a medium saucepan, melt the butter over medium heat. Whisk in the cocoa powder, cinnamon, chipotle powder, and salt. Cook, whisking, for 3 minutes. Whisk in the milk and powdered sugar until smooth, then add the vanilla. Stir in the chopped pecans.

5. While the cake is very hot from the oven, pour the glaze over the entire cake, spreading it evenly.

6. Cool completely before serving. Slice the cake in a 5-by-5 grid to create 25 servings.

Make Ahead: Store the cake in the refrigerator tightly wrapped in plastic for up to 1 week. Before serving, either bring it to room temperature on the counter or place it in a warm oven for a couple of minutes.

A Guide to the Perfect Backyard Bar Setup

When I'm throwing a large casual party, I always encourage guests to contribute to the bar spread. This not only saves you on having to provide for everyone, but also allows for variety. It sparks conversation. You might learn something new about a friend based on their beverage contribution. But regardless of what your guests bring, you should always provide a good base. Here are my essentials:

Drinkware

I have a stash of 15 to 20 inexpensive stackable glasses that I use for parties with less than 20 guests. If the party is bigger than that, I go disposable (but recyclable). A good rule of thumb for glassware is to stock 1½ times the number of expected guests. Someone will inevitably misplace, discard, or break a glass and end up taking another.

Cocktail Napkins

If it's a small group coming over, then I pull out the small linen cocktail napkins. They're inexpensive, reusable, easy to source, and let's face it: nice. For large parties, I go for paper, but I still go for something cute.

Beverage Vessel

I have a big vintage sink, pulled out of a Brooklyn warehouse dumpster that's mounted to the wall in my backyard specifically for ice and beverages. But if you, for some reason, don't have that, a cooler or big bowl works well, too. Either way, have a smaller cooler or bucket set aside for drinking ice, along with a scoop or tongs. Do not underestimate the dramatic power of a vintage ice bucket.

Ice

Enough ice to fill your beverage bucket twice. Honestly, a midparty ice run is also a nice break if you live within walking distance of a grocery or corner store that sells ice. Have plenty of ice, it will keep the party rolling.

Wine Keys and Bottle Openers

Have at least two wine keys and/or bottle openers at the bar. If any of your friends are service industry folks, someone will inevitably pocket one out of sheer muscle memory, so have extra.

Beverage

A good rule of thumb is one drink, per guest, per hour. More if your crowd is, ahem, thirsty.

Water

Hydration is key! Don't make your guests have to ask for water or go searching in your kitchen for a glass to fill at the tap. Set up a little station that's easily accessible with pitchers of ice water and a stack of glasses. Some sliced lemon or fresh mint snuck in there is a nice touch. If table space is an issue, throw a case or two of bottles in the cooler.

The Soft Stuff

I've got more and more nondrinkers in my circle and I never want to make them feel like an afterthought. I always throw a case of Mexican Coke and some fancy seltzers in the mix. And a chilled bottle of your favorite zero-proof aperitivo next to a dish of sliced citrus makes for an inviting spritz station.

Wine

Stock a couple of easy crowd-pleasers; moderately priced, but something to go with the food and sunshine. I always have a couple whites, rosés, and chilled reds in my early-summer cooler. Guests will likely contribute, so make sure your beverage vessel has breathing room!

Beer

Grab a case of your favorite easy drinker: Think of it as a neutral, something of a backdrop. This is the "starter pack," not something to carry the party. Someone can always run out for more if the party keeps going! I go for the classics. There are some great nonalcoholic beers on the market, too!

2+ WEEKS OUT

Send invites out at least 2 weeks in advance of your party, if not more. Being the first party starts with being the first party announced.

6 DAYS OUT

Clean up your yard, patio, alley, or whatever space you plan to host in. A couple of fresh potted plants go a long way in making a grass patch feel like a garden.

Purchase propane or charcoal, plus a backup.

5 DAYS OUT

Inventory your pantry, taking note of any staple ingredients you're missing. Don't forget essentials like aluminum foil, food wrap, zip-seal bags, paper towels, storage containers, trash bags, kitchen tape, and a marker.

Purchase paper products, beverages, nonperishable ingredients, and the ingredients for your sauces.

4 DAYS OUT

Make all three sauces and store them in the fridge.

3 DAYS OUT

Clean the house. Even for an outdoor party, folks will likely be inside. A clean bathroom with a pleasant candle and extra toilet paper are a party must. And the first part of your prep is giving yourself an organized, clean kitchen.

2 DAYS OUT

Shop for all the perishable items.

Make the marinades for the meat and veggies; store the vinegary one in the fridge.

Trim the ribs, slather with marinade, and put them to bed in the fridge.

Make the Blue Cheese Green Goddess dressing.

Soak the beans.

1 DAY OUT

Roast off the ribs, chill them overnight.

Marinate the chicken.

Slice the veggies for the All Green Slaw. Store the asparagus ribbons and spears in water in the fridge. The rest, put into airtight containers, covered with a damp paper towel.

Make the Drawn Butter Vinaigrette.

Finish the Root Beer Beans, chill them overnight (they'll be even better!).

Make the pie dough, wrap tightly, and refrigerate.

Make the sheet cake. If you wrap it tightly, no one will be able to tell it was baked the day before.

6 HOURS OUT

Assemble and bake the pie.

Cut and marinate the zucchini.

4 HOURS OUT

Make the punch and chill.

Chill the wine and beer.

Do a final tidy of the house and outdoor space.

1 HOUR OUT

Cover the beans and warm them in a 300°F oven.

Boil the potatoes for the salad.

30 MINUTES OUT

Set up a bar (or make someone else do it).

Light the grill.

Put on your favorite playlist.

Pour yourself a drink: It'll help you look at ease when guests arrive, even if you don't feel it.

Put out snacks. Even though you've obviously followed this schedule to the minute, snacks will help buffer while you're grilling.

THE PARTY BEGINS

Greet your guests, who have arrived perfectly on time.

Dress the salads.

Grill (and chill).

PLAN AHEAD

In the Garden

WITH BRAD OGBONNA

Professionally, Brad is a photographer and director. But he is also well-known for his involvement at Prima Brooklyn coffee shop and wine bar, hosting soirées in his garden, and being the go-to home cook in his friend group. His recipes marry the Igbo cuisine he grew up with and flavors he experiences when traveling the world for work.

I grew up in a close-knit community where food always felt bountiful and communal. My mom loved to cook, and my dad loved to host, so almost every weekend was spent gathering at home, either ours or our family's or a friend's.

STEAL
MY
PLAYLIST

As I've gotten older, I've tried to hold on to those same traditions as much as possible, thinking of myself as a hybrid of the cook and the host. In my twenties, I would throw BBQs and parties on my Brooklyn rooftop, and now into my thirties I've graduated to cozy, intimate indoor dinner parties in the winter and more lavish garden parties in my backyard in the warmer months.

My career is in photography, which takes me on the road a lot. A fortunate side effect of traveling so much for work is that I get to experience cultures and cuisines from every corner of the world. The dishes I've tasted, the people I've shared food with, and the ways in which we've gathered together have all shaped my palate and hosting style immensely. So, when I do get a moment at home, I love to have people together, catch up, and share the things I've picked up along the way.

One of the most memorable meals I've ever had was at La Chassagnette in Arles, France. I was blown away by the high-concept menu and dishes made with locally grown ingredients, many of which came right from the restaurant's garden. Despite it being a Michelin star restaurant, it felt so unpretentious and more like we were enjoying an afternoon at a friend's house. I have always loved the idea of long, lazy lunches with decadent spreads. I felt transported to an old Éric Rohmer film where the summers were idyllic and meals were a central part of the day, lasting for hours. It is this exact spirit I want to capture when June rolls around and it's time—finally—for my garden dinner party.

I've always liked to think of my space as a meeting point for friends and family to come and share a meal or drink. My garden has become an oasis in the midst of the bustling city not just for myself, but for my community as well. There's something undeniably refreshing about dining al fresco, especially at the homestead where you can create an environment that's relaxed, unhurried, and brimming with intentionality. June feels like the opening of the season: It's finally warm again and people are in good spirits. The garden is just getting going, so with each new day there's something growing. I always want to incorporate at least one ingredient from the garden into whatever dishes I plan on serving. The promise of food will always be a draw, but the vibes are just as important—from the drinks (think: natural, light, effervescent wines and vermouths) to the music (eclectic and upbeat). Everything works in tandem.

I don't have any formal background in food or cooking, I simply enjoy doing it. It makes me feel connected to my upbringing and my culinary heritage, and provides me an opportunity to share those parts of myself with the people around me. It's an opportunity for me to be present in the garden, with the ingredients, with my local fishmonger, and with the people I have the honor of feeding that day. In a season of life where my days are packed and I move around a lot, the garden party is a chance to slow down and enjoy simplicity and fun. Hosting should be just that: simple and fun. Let the privacy of your home be its own kind of oasis where time is elastic, cooking is entertaining, and conversation abounds.

Sweet Vermouth Spritz

Makes 1 drink

Nothing is more enjoyable than a chilled spritz during the warmer months. I think it is the perfect drink to offer guests upon arrival before people start exploring the wine selection. It's an easygoing cocktail alternative with a lower ABV to start folks off on a nice, slow, sweet, and tart note. The choice of sweet vermouth is classic and unexpected, and it doesn't take much to make this spritz shine. Just add some effervescence and lemon zest and people will think you've performed a miracle. You can use either sparkling water or a not-too-expensive sparkling wine like Cava or prosecco to provide the sparkle.

2 ounces sweet vermouth
4 ounces soda water, Cava, or prosecco
Ice
Lemon zest and peel

Mix the vermouth and bubbles of your choosing together in an ice-filled tumbler glass. Stir in a touch of lemon zest and garnish with a thumb-length strip of lemon peel.

What's in Season

Growing your own food can be as unpredictable as it is rewarding. June is the early days of summer in New York, and every year looks a little different. Whether I'm able to source directly from my backyard or I make a trip to the farmers' market, here are the ingredients most likely to be sprouting and ready for the taking this time of year:

Arugula	Fava beans	Radishes
Kale	Garlic scapes	Shallots
Broccoli	Kohlrabi	Summer squash
Swiss chard	Snap peas	Tomatoes
Chives	Rhubarb	Zucchini

Spicy Steamed Oysters

Serves 4

I discovered pretty late in life that I enjoy oysters, so I've been making up for lost time by always saying YES to oysters. This recipe brings me back to a trip to Charleston, South Carolina. It was there that I tried steamed oysters for the first time and was blown away by how the texture and taste of the oyster evolved when introduced to heat. I love adding a little kick to the freshness of the oysters with a little spicy pepper to a traditional mignonette sauce that you can serve alongside the oysters.

Preparing oysters at home can feel intimidating, but once you get the hang of using an oyster shucker, it almost becomes a way of life. For this particular recipe, the heat will actually be doing most of the work to open up the oysters, but you can use the same spicy mignonette for fresh oysters as well.

I personally prefer East Coast oysters, which I find to have a savory brininess and overall higher salinity and minerality. The meat is often a little more chewy and solid than the West Coast oysters, and fare better with heat. However, the world is your oyster as they say! Feel free to work with what you have available!

Spicy Mignonette
½ habanero pepper, finely diced
1 small shallot, finely diced
1 tablespoon finely chopped fresh cilantro
¼ cup fresh lime juice (1 to 2 limes)
Small pinch of salt
Small pinch of sugar

12 fresh oysters
Flaky sea salt

1. Make the spicy mignonette: In a small bowl, mix together the habanero, shallot, cilantro, lime juice, salt, and sugar. Let sit for 30 minutes.

2. Scrub the oysters well to remove any excess mud and sand grit. Rinse with only cold water and do not leave your oysters to sit in water at any point.

3. In a large, deep pan, bring 1 inch of water to a boil. Meanwhile, place the oysters cup side down in a steamer basket that can fit in or over the pan without touching the water. Do not stack the oysters; if they do not all fit in the basket, steam them in batches.

4. Once the water is boiling, place the steamer basket in/over the pan and cover it with the lid. Steam the oysters until the shells just begin to open, 5 to 7 minutes. Carefully remove from the steamer from the pan and set aside.

5. Discard the top shells of the oysters and lay them on a platter. Spoon a little of the mignonette sauce over the oysters, sprinkle with flaky sea salt, and serve on the half shell.

Spicy Nigerian Tomato Stew

Serves 6 to 8

I grew up with a lot of Nigerian cuisine: soups and stews, grilled meats and vegetables, and many different types of rice dishes. Out of all of them, though, this is the one I return to the most. It's a staple in almost every home and restaurant around Nigeria and parts of West Africa. It tastes like home and reminds me of my family and our history, and is relatively easy to make. Traditionally, it's served with rice and plantain, but is also served for breakfast alongside scrambled eggs. One of my fondest memories is making this on the weekends with my dad—we always had the sauce on hand.

You can add any type of cooked protein to the stew or leave it as is. I like to add a meaty white fish, like red snapper, branzino, or cod, but chicken, beef, lamb, and goat are all great, too. I like to make it in big batches and have it on deck for when I decide to have guests over or just need a quick meal on demand. It keeps very well in the freezer.

9 plum or Roma tomatoes (3½ to 4 pounds), seeded and chopped

3 large red bell peppers, chopped

3 to 4 Scotch bonnet or habanero peppers, seeded and chopped (adjust the heat according to your spice tolerance)

1 head garlic, halved horizontally

2-inch knob fresh ginger, peeled and chopped

2 large red or white onions, thinly sliced

Olive oil

Kosher salt and freshly ground black pepper

½ cup neutral oil, such as grapeseed, vegetable, or avocado oil

One 12-ounce can tomato paste

1¾ cups beef stock

1 teaspoon curry powder

1 teaspoon onion powder

2 teaspoons dried thyme

2 teaspoons bouillon powder or paste, or 1 cube

2 meaty white fish fillets (1 pound each), such as red snapper, branzino, or cod

1. Preheat the oven to 350°F.

2. Place the tomatoes, bell peppers, hot peppers, garlic, ginger, and half of the onion slices on your Oven Pan. Toss with a healthy drizzle of olive oil and season with salt and black pepper.

3. Roast the vegetables for 30 to 40 minutes, until they look well done all around and have some color. This will give the dish a deep smoky flavor. When the vegetables are cool enough to handle, transfer to a blender and puree until smooth. Set aside.

4. Meanwhile, in a large pot, heat the neutral oil over medium heat. Add the tomato paste and remaining sliced onions and cook until caramelized, 10 to 12 minutes.

5. Stir in the blended pepper/tomato mixture, cover, and leave to cook over low heat for about 10 minutes. Stir to prevent burning.

6. Stir in the stock, curry powder, onion powder, thyme, and bouillon. Cover the stew and cook over low heat for about 1 hour to allow the flavors to marry.

7. Cut the fillets into 2-inch pieces. Add the fish to the simmering stew, cover, and cook until cooked through, 6 to 8 minutes depending on the fish. (If using another precooked protein like roasted chicken, add it to the stew 20 minutes before serving.) Season with salt and black pepper to taste.

Zanzibari Octopus Curry

Serves 6 to 8

In 2019, during the height of a miserable winter in Minneapolis, I was scrolling through Instagram and saw a friend post these incredible videos from somewhere warm and surely far, far away. I was struck with envy and decided wherever it was, I was going to go that following week. So, just like that, I took an impromptu trip to Stone Town, Zanzibar, a small island off the coast of Tanzania. It took a few flights and a two-hour ferry ride, but it was all worth it. I was immediately blown away by the natural beauty of the island and its unique mixture of cultures—East African, Arab, and Asian— that seemed to cohabitate in harmony.

Every morning I'd watch as the locals made their way to the ocean, each returning with the fresh catch of the day. In the evenings there was a large food bazaar in a park by the water with stalls upon stalls. The octopus curry was prolific, such a common dish you'd see it on every menu whether at the bazaar to a fancy hotel. It is a clear representation of Stone Town, from its distinctly salty sea flavors to its balance of spices. This dish can be enjoyed alone or with rice or chapati.

First time working with octopus? Here are some tips: Ask your fishmonger to tenderize it for you. Also ask them to help remove the beak—you won't regret it.

One 2-pound octopus

2 tablespoons vegetable oil

2 carrots, diced

1 white onion, diced

3 garlic cloves, minced

2-inch knob fresh ginger, minced

2 hot chiles, seeded and diced

2 tomatoes, seeded and diced

1 tablespoon ground coriander

2 tablespoons ground turmeric

1 tablespoon baharat spice blend

Juice of 2 limes (3 to 4 tablespoons)

2½ cups full-fat coconut milk, canned (1½ cans) or fresh (from 2 to 4 coconuts)

Kosher salt and freshly ground black pepper

Handful of fresh cilantro, finely chopped

1. Bring a large pot of water to a boil over medium heat. Add the octopus and cook, uncovered, for 15 minutes (if you have an octopus heavier than 2 pounds, for each additional pound of octopus, add 3 to 5 minutes). Remove from the heat and allow to rest for 15 to 20 minutes with the pot covered.

2. Transfer to a large cutting board. Cut the tentacles into small chunks and cube the head. For the tentacle pieces, use a paring knife to remove the purplish outer skin layer, leaving only the white circle of meat within.

3. In a nonstick pan, warm the vegetable oil over medium heat. Add the carrots, onion, garlic, ginger, and chiles and cook until softened, 5 to 6 minutes. Add the octopus, stir to coat, and simmer for 3 minutes.

4. Add the tomatoes, coriander, turmeric, baharat spice blend, and half the lime juice. Simmer, uncovered, for 5 minutes to reduce slightly. Add the coconut milk and simmer for another 5 minutes. Add the remaining lime juice and bring to a boil. Reduce the heat and simmer until the octopus is cooked through and the flavors marry, about 45 minutes.

5. Season with salt and pepper to taste and top with the cilantro.

A VISIT TO THE FISHMONGER

9:08 A.M. SHIPWRECK, BROOKLYN
It's the morning of your dinner party. Everything has been bought and prepped except the seafood. You're here to get the freshest ingredients possible, while they're still in stock.

> BRAD
>
> I'm hosting a dinner party in my garden, and hoping to make seafood the star of the show. What's fresh and in season?

> FISHMONGER
>
> Got a shipment of Chilean sea bass. Perfect for June.

> BRAD
>
> Beautiful. Mind if I take a closer look?

Brad checks the gills. If they've been removed, it's probably an older fish. They should be purple or red. Brad also takes a whiff. Trust your nose. If it's super fishy, it's likely past its prime.

> BRAD
>
> This looks great. Could you go ahead and skin two fillets for me?

> FISHMONGER
>
> You got it. Anything else?

> BRAD
>
> Yep! I need an octopus. Would you mind removing the beak for me? And, let's tenderize it while you're at it.

> FISHMONGER
>
> You're lucky, we just got a fresh shipment. Otherwise, I'd say frozen is always better than thawed.

> BRAD
>
> So true. Last up, I need some oysters. Medium and with a nice brine, if you have it.

> FISHMONGER
>
> I've got these ones from Maine on ice. Here, check it out. Nice and heavy, super fresh.

Brad knows that oysters need to be on ice, heavy with the brine or "liquor," and consumed the day they're purchased.

> BRAD
>
> I'll take a dozen. Thanks!

Suya-Crusted Whole Fish

Serves 6 to 8

Suya is a traditional smoky and spicy seasoning that originated in Northern Nigeria, but spread to surrounding areas. Suya is synonymous with street food across West Africa. Anytime you go out at night in countries like Ghana or Nigeria, you'll see suya stands all over with people lining up to get some. It's smoky, nutty, and spicy, and much like most ingredients in this region, there's no one way to make it or enjoy it. Everyone has their own particular twist, which is what makes trying multiple versions of the same food so interesting. For this particular recipe, I lend the suya spice to a whole fish instead of the usual grilled meat, but feel free to use the leftover suya spice to try on lamb, goat, chicken, or beef skewers as well.

One of my favorite dishes to make for friends is a whole fish. I grew up in Minnesota and did not eat fish for most of my life until I moved to New York City. At first, I was intimidated by cooking fish, but I soon realized it's one of the quickest things to prepare and there's so much you can do with it.

Suya Spice Blend

1 cup roasted unsalted peanuts

1½ teaspoons smoked paprika

1 teaspoon cayenne pepper

1 teaspoon garlic powder

½ teaspoon onion powder

¼ teaspoon ground ginger

1 teaspoon chicken bouillon powder,
   or ½ cube

Fish

1 whole meaty white fish (1½ to 2 pounds),
   such as branzino or red snapper

4 tablespoons olive oil

2 teaspoons salt

1 lemon, sliced

A few sprigs of parsley and cilantro

2 tablespoons butter

½ red onion, diced, for serving

1. Preheat the oven to 400°F.

2. Make the suya spice blend: In a medium pan, lightly toast the peanuts. Let them cool, then transfer to a food processor and process until they're powdery.

3. Add the smoked paprika, cayenne, garlic powder, onion powder, ginger, and bouillon powder and process to blend.

4. Prepare the fish: Cut three slits into the fish on both sides. Rub the fish with 2 tablespoons of the olive oil and season with the salt. Rub the fish with the suya spice blend, reserving some spice for serving, and press lightly to ensure it's entirely coated. Stuff the cavity with some lemon slices and the herbs.

5. Preheat a cast-iron pan over medium-high heat for a couple minutes. Add the butter and remaining 2 tablespoons oil and heat until they shimmer. Add the fish and cook undisturbed until a blackened crust forms and it loosens from the pan, about 6 minutes.

6. Gently flip the fish and transfer to the oven. Bake until the internal temperature reaches 145°F, 10 to 15 minutes.

7. Remove the fish from the oven and allow it to rest before serving with more lemon slices, the diced red onion, and additional suya spice blend to taste.

Spicy Kale, Tomato, Pepper & Onion Slaw

Serves 6 to 8

This dish was a staple in my mom's kitchen. Simple and really flavorful. A great side dish to any protein and rice, or even just enjoyed alone. I prefer to use dinosaur kale, but any leafy green will do! As with most dishes, the fresher the ingredients the better.

1 to 2 tablespoons olive oil

1 red or white onion, thinly sliced

3 garlic cloves, thinly sliced

1 to 2 habanero or Scotch bonnet peppers (depending on your spice tolerance), thinly sliced

1 red bell pepper, thinly sliced

1 plum tomato, diced

1 bunch of dinosaur kale (aka Tuscan or lacinato), thinly sliced (trim stems where they're extra stalky)

½ cube chicken bouillon

Kosher salt and freshly ground black pepper

1. In a medium pan, heat the olive oil over medium heat. Add the onion and sweat for 5 minutes. Add the garlic, hot peppers, bell pepper, and tomato and cook together until they have some color, 5 to 7 minutes.

2. Add the kale, bouillon, and 1 cup water. Cover and stir periodically over low heat until the kale is soft, about 10 minutes. Uncover and simmer for 5 minutes to reduce the liquid. Taste and adjust the seasoning with salt and black pepper.

Basil-Infused Olive Oil

Makes about 2½ cups

1. Set up a bowl of ice and water. In a saucepan, bring 4 cups salted water to a boil. Add one bunch of fresh basil and blanch for 5 seconds. Drain and immediately plunge into the ice bath. Once cooled, drain and pat the leaves dry with a paper towel.

2. In a food processor, puree the basil with 2 cups of olive oil. Season with salt and pepper.

3. Strain the basil oil through a fine-mesh sieve and discard the basil remnants. Pour the oil into a jar, cover, and refrigerate until ready to use. Basil oil will keep this way in the fridge for up to 2 weeks. Bring to room temperature before serving.

Sautéed Sugar Snap Pea Salad

Serves 6 to 8

This is one of my ultimate summer salads! So much of it can be grown in the garden and has a great balance of fresh ingredients to keep it interesting while still very light.

Dressing

3 white anchovy fillets (boquerones)

1 small shallot, diced

1 garlic clove, chopped

Grated zest and juice of 1 large lemon

Sea salt and freshly ground black pepper

Salad

½ pound sugar snap peas, halved lengthwise, stringy pieces removed

Olive oil

1 bunch of watermelon radishes, French breakfast radishes, or regular radishes, thinly sliced (about 2 cups)

1 cup pea shoots

One 5-ounce box arugula

Six 2-ounce burrata balls (or three 4-ounce balls)

4 tablespoons Basil-Infused Olive Oil (recipe opposite)

Sea salt and freshly ground black pepper

Lemon wedges, for squeezing

1. Make the dressing: In a small bowl, combine the anchovies, shallot, garlic, lemon zest, and lemon juice and season with salt and lots of black pepper.

2. Make the salad: In a pan, cook the sugar snap peas with a little olive oil over medium heat until slightly softened, about 6 minutes. Let them cool.

3. In a large salad bowl, combine the sugar snaps, radishes, pea shoots, and arugula. Mix in the dressing a couple of minutes before serving and top with sliced-open burrata balls. Finish with a drizzle of the basil-infused olive oil, a sprinkle of salt and pepper, and a squeeze of lemon.

Summer Squash Pasta

Serves 6 to 8

As a gardener, I am a big believer in the phrase "If it grows together, it goes together." There is no proof more obvious than in a simple summer vegetable pasta. Choose an exciting pasta shape, use your good olive oil, and break out the fancy aged Parmesan, and you're set.

Salt

1 pound farfalle or reginetti pasta

1 fresh baguette

¼ cup extra-virgin olive oil, plus more for drizzling

Freshly ground black pepper

2 cups cherry tomatoes

3 garlic cloves, thinly sliced

¼ teaspoon red pepper flakes

1 yellow zucchini, cut into chunky half-rounds

1 green zucchini, cut into chunky half-rounds

1¼ cups freshly grated Parmesan cheese, plus more for serving

Juice of 1 lemon

¼ cup chopped fresh basil, plus leaves for garnish

1. Preheat the oven to 350°F.

2. Meanwhile, bring salted water to a boil in your Perfect Pot. Add the pasta and cook to al dente according to the package directions. Drain well.

3. Tear the baguette into medium chunks, then drizzle some olive oil, salt, and black pepper on them. Spread on a sheet pan and bake until golden brown, about 15 minutes. Remove from the oven and set the croutons aside to cool. Leave the oven on.

4. Slice the cherry tomatoes in half, drizzle with some olive oil, and season with salt to taste. Arrange them on the sheet pan and bake until just blistered, about 15 minutes. Take the tomatoes out of the oven and let them cool.

5. In a nonstick pan, heat the ¼ cup olive oil over medium to medium-high heat. Once hot, add the garlic and pepper flakes and sauté for 30 seconds to 1 minute. Add the zucchini and sauté until tender, 4 to 5 minutes. Season with salt and pepper.

6. Add the cooked pasta and roasted tomatoes and toss with the zucchini mixture. Add the Parmesan cheese, croutons, lemon juice, and chopped basil, then season to taste with additional salt and pepper. Serve with more Parmesan, basil leaves, and finishing oil as needed.

Spicy & Sweet Flatbread

Serves 6 to 8

This is one of my favorite things to eat with fresh fish or grilled chicken. Something about it feels like summer to me. I developed this recipe after a visit to the restaurant ÖTAP in Brussels and I enjoyed it so much that I had to immediately add it to the repertoire. It's no surprise that it's always a big hit. The fun part of this dish is dressing up the flatbread with various fresh or dried herbs—so feel free to get creative with what you have available.

2 to 2⅓ cups all-purpose or bread flour

1 envelope instant (rapid-rise) yeast (2¼ teaspoons)

1½ teaspoons sugar

¾ teaspoon kosher salt

¼ teaspoon garlic powder

¼ teaspoon dried basil

¼ teaspoon dried thyme or rosemary

2 tablespoons extra-virgin olive oil, plus more for greasing

¾ cup warm water

1 tablespoon Calabrian chile oil or other spicy chile oil, plus more for drizzling

1 tablespoon honey (Mike's Hot Honey if you have it)

1 tablespoon za'atar

Fresh rosemary, for garnish (optional)

1. In a large bowl, combine 1 cup of the flour, the yeast, sugar, salt, garlic powder, and dried herbs. Add the olive oil and warm water and use a wooden spoon to stir well to combine. Gradually add another 1 cup of the flour, stirring until the dough forms into a cohesive, elastic ball and begins to pull away from the sides of the bowl. The dough should be slightly sticky but manageable with your hands. If the dough is too wet and unmanageably sticky and more flour is needed, work it in a little at a time until the right consistency is achieved.

2. Drizzle a separate large clean bowl generously with olive oil and use a pastry brush to bring the oil up the sides of the bowl. Lightly dust your hands with flour, form the dough into a round ball, and transfer to the bowl. Use your hands to roll the dough along the inside of the bowl until it is coated in olive oil. Cover the bowl tightly with plastic wrap and leave it in a warm place to rise until it has doubled in size, about 30 minutes.

3. Preheat the oven to 425°F. Line a pizza pan or sheet pan with parchment paper.

4. Use your hands to gently deflate the dough and transfer it to a lightly floured surface. Knead briefly until smooth, 3 to 5 times. Use either your hands or a rolling pin to work the dough into a 12-inch round. Transfer the dough to the lined pan. Drizzle the dough with Calabrian chile oil or any other spicy oil, using your pastry brush to coat the entire surface of the flatbread with the oil. Use a fork to poke holes all over the center of the flatbread to keep the dough from bubbling up in the oven.

5. Bake until a light gold crust forms, 10 to 13 minutes.

6. Remove from the oven and let cool for 1 minute. Add the honey and za'atar and drizzle with more spicy oil. Garnish with rosemary or any other fresh herbs if desired.

Wine Sourcing

While I can always rely on my friends to show up with a bottle or two in tow, I also like to have a healthy selection on hand when I host. (Full disclosure: I run a wine bar in Brooklyn called Prima on the side, so to say I "like" wine is a bit of an understatement.) June is the perfect time of year to break out my personal favorites: Natural wines with lots of character. Light- to medium-bodied, dry, slightly or full-on effervescent, fruity or floral, macerated whites and chilled reds, unrefined and funky. All in all, unconventional yet timely wines.

One of the benefits of eating and drinking with a larger group is that you get to try more wines than you would alone. I recommend seizing this opportunity and creating a diverse yet cohesive wine selection to carry you through the party. I like to grab something chilled, something effervescent, something funky, something light, and something red.

6 DAYS OUT

Send your invite texts.

Secure the wine and/or assign your guests a wine type to help you stock the bar.

Call your fishmonger and order an octopus that is already cleaned and tenderized to be picked up before your dinner party.

3 DAYS OUT

Make the Spicy Nigerian Tomato Stew, but hold back the protein. Store in an airtight container in the refrigerator.

Make the suya spice and store in an airtight container in the refrigerator.

2 DAYS OUT

Buy flowers and herbs.

Make the spicy mignonette for the oysters and store in an airtight container in the refrigerator.

1 DAY OUT

Make the flatbread dough, wrap it tightly in plastic wrap, and store in the refrigerator.

Make the Zanzibari Octopus Curry and store in an airtight container in the refrigerator.

Make the Spicy Kale, Tomato, Pepper & Onion Slaw and store in an airtight container in the refrigerator.

Sweep the garden.

 ### DINNER PARTY!

Go to the fishmonger in the morning to get the oysters and fish.

PREP ORDER

Preheat the oven to 350°F for the croutons and tomatoes, and later the Suya-Crusted Whole Fish.

Prep the Sautéed Snap Pea Salad, but don't toss everything together until just before serving.

Prep the Pasta Salad. Roast the croutons and tomatoes. Sauté the squash and hold in the pan. Have a pot of water coming to a boil for the pasta.

Reheat on the stovetop:

> Tomato Stew
> Octopus Curry
> Slaw

Increase the oven temperature to 400°F and rub the fish with the suya spice.

Sear the fish and place in the oven.

Roll out the dough for the flatbread.

Bake off the flatbread once the fish is cooked.

Finish the tomato stew with protein.

Cook the pasta and toss with the rest of the pasta ingredients.

Steam the oysters.

Toss the salad ingredients together.

Serve it all!

Dinner Is the Destination

WITH GERARDO GONZALEZ

From the downtown Manhattan kitchens of El Rey and Lalito to overseeing culinary programming at Palm Heights hotel in Grand Cayman, Gerardo's cooking practice draws inspiration from his surroundings and travels. With a laid-back approach to hosting, Gerardo is an expert in using local flavors in his recipes and adjusting for last-minute plus-ones.

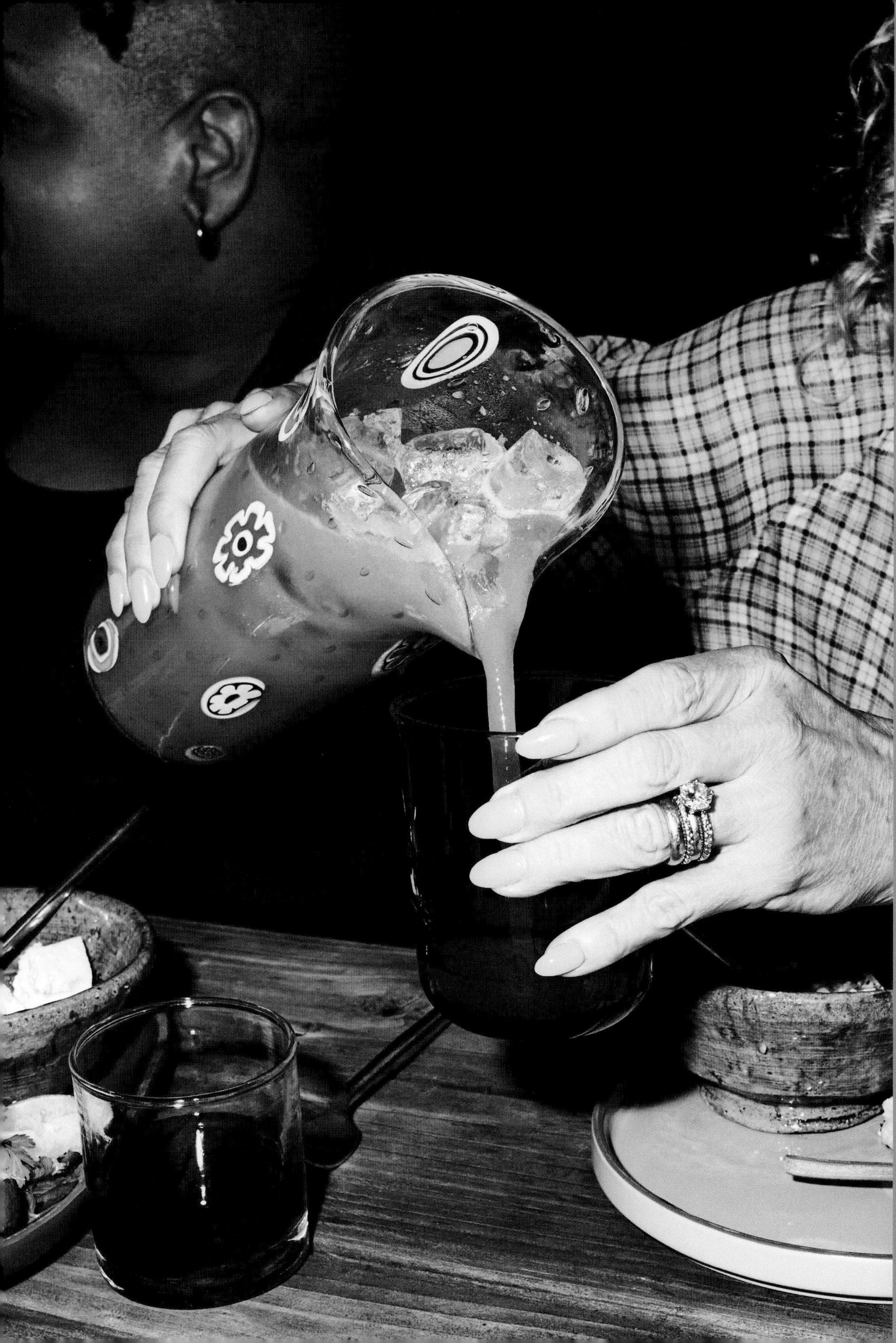

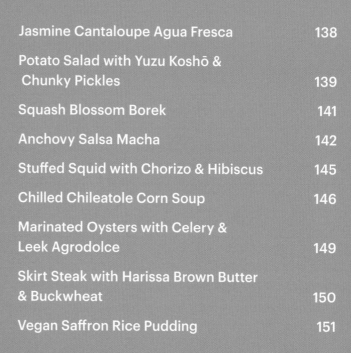

July is my favorite month of the year, and for good reason. It combines two of the most important things to me as a cook—peak produce and travel—which also happen to be the guiding principles of this dinner party.

STEAL MY PLAYLIST

One of the best ways to get to know a new place is to explore the local markets, farms, and spice shops, and there's really no better time of year to do it. I don't know about you, but I find that I and everyone I know are always off traveling this time of year. So, with your normal dinner party crew dispersed, July makes the perfect month to take your dinner party on the road . . . at least in spirit. Whatever your month holds—a road trip to a nearby town, a flight to a far-off destination, or just a venture to a new grocer or market in your city—there's something about this time of year that drives us to explore. Whether you decide to host over your travels or to set up shop in your own backyard, this dinner party works best if you approach it with a traveler's curiosity. It's all about discovering new flavors and forging new relationships, all while finding inventive, beautiful ways of eating and gathering together.

Fresh produce doesn't just define my cooking, but also where I choose to live and work. Nothing makes me want to host more than when the farmers' markets are brimming with the best of the season. There's such an abundance that having a dinner party only makes sense—I can't possibly eat everything I want to cook on my own, so it's the perfect excuse to invite friends and family over to share a meal. I love planning the menu around the ingredients and finding ways to incorporate them into dishes so that their natural flavors take center stage. With this menu—and any dish you're making—don't worry if you can't find an ingredient you were planning on using. July is one of the best months to try new things with a variety of options. Ask around, sample as much as you can, and use this time

to swap out for something similar, but different. You might just find a new favorite thing to look forward to.

While the menu is first and foremost a celebration of the ingredients (I love July produce, if you haven't been able to tell), it is also an ode to the people, places, and meals that have defined my travels. The recipes are inspired by some of the most memorable dishes I've tasted over the years.

For me, the gathering doesn't start when the food is set at the table. I find that folks love to be part of the process in planning (if you are willing). Invite someone to go to the market and help you select the ingredients. Happily task them to help in the kitchen; I like to have specific things set aside to assign to people should they offer to help. If they'd rather not be a part of the cooking, make them feel equally involved by passing them the duties like managing the music while you're cooking or sitting down to eat. Ask them to set the table, or make sure you have enough chairs, or set up the bar. Who is in the kitchen is as important as who's at the table. Making the process part of the event will make your dinner party that much more memorable and enjoyable.

Let July be a month of celebration and joy. Use it as your excuse to gather with loved ones at the homestead or on the road. Throw your first dinner party abroad. Invite someone you just met. Let the seasonal abundance inspire new and exciting dishes you've never tried. Let the cooking be half the party. Fire up the grill, sample all of the produce, and get ready to create memories that will last a lifetime.

Jasmine Cantaloupe Agua Fresca

Serves 6

I love making aguas frescas this time of year. They are the perfect format for your farmers' market haul to shine, and they tend to be crowd-pleasers. I love centering melon, a deeply underappreciated fruit, but feel free to experiment with your favorite fruity flavors of the summer.

½ cup sugar

½ cup dried jasmine flowers

2 medium cantaloupes, peeled, seeded, and cut into pieces

½ cup fresh lemon juice

Ice

1. In a medium saucepan, combine the sugar and 1 cup water and bring to a boil, stirring until the sugar is dissolved. Remove from the heat and let cool for a few minutes.

2. Add the dried jasmine flowers to a jar with an airtight lid. Pour the simple syrup in over the flowers and let steep in the refrigerator overnight.

3. In a blender, puree the cantaloupe with 2 cups water and the lemon juice until smooth. Strain the jasmine flowers from the simple syrup and reserve. Add the syrup to the cantaloupe puree. Stir well to combine.

4. Serve the cantaloupe jasmine agua fresca over ice, garnishing each glass with 2 buds of the soaked jasmine flowers.

Potato Salad with Yuzu Koshō & Chunky Pickles

Serves 8 to 10

Enjoy this unique twist on classic potato salad with the zesty, citrusy flavor of yuzu koshō and the tanginess of full sour pickles. If yuzu koshō isn't available at your local Asian supermarket, swap it out for any chile paste and add some citrus zest yourself. If you're having fewer people over, this recipe can be easily halved.

Kosher salt

6 cups extra-large diced Yukon Gold potatoes

1 cup coarsely diced celery

1 cup mayonnaise

½ cup diced white onion

2 teaspoons yuzu koshō

1 tablespoon fresh lemon juice

1½ teaspoons freshly ground black pepper

3 cups thickly sliced full-sour pickles, plus more for garnish

½ cup chopped fresh parsley, plus more for garnish

1. Bring a pot of heavily salted water to a boil. Add the potatoes and cook until soft and easily smashable, about 15 minutes. Drain and set aside to cool.

2. In a large bowl, combine the cooled potatoes, celery, mayonnaise, onion, yuzu koshō, lemon juice, and black pepper. Stir until well combined. Fold in the pickles, being careful not to break them up too much. Cover the bowl with plastic wrap and refrigerate for at least 1 hour to let the flavors meld together.

3. Before serving, stir in the parsley and add salt to taste. Serve chilled with additional full-sour pickles and parsley for garnish.

Squash Blossom Borek

Serves 6

Borek—a spiraled, flaky, phyllo pie—is a perfect vessel for endless combinations of ingredients and flavors. Treat it as the base for whatever produce catches your eye at the market (or needs to be retired from your fridge). This particular borek puts peak summer squash and hearty chard at its center, but you should feel at liberty to let whatever sturdy summer vegetables (eggplant or peppers, for example) you want to shine in this dish. If you're enjoying this recipe as a main, serve it alongside spicy arugula dressed with olive oil and lemon juice.

Filling

3 tablespoons olive oil

1½ cups finely diced summer squash

½ cup diced chard stems

Kosher salt and freshly ground black pepper

2 cups chopped rainbow chard leaves

¾ cup sliced squash blossoms

2 tablespoons fresh lemon juice

1 cup crumbled feta cheese, preferably sheep's milk

½ cup ricotta cheese

¼ cup grated goat Gouda cheese

Grated zest of 1 lemon

Assembly

Olive oil, for the pan

7 sheets phyllo dough

1 cup ghee or butter, melted

Egg wash: 1 egg yolk beaten with 1 tablespoon milk

1. Make the filling: In a medium nonstick pan, heat 2 tablespoons of the olive oil over medium heat. Add the squash and sauté until slightly softened but still al dente, about 5 minutes. Add the chard stems, season with salt and pepper, and cook until tender, about 3 minutes. Add the chard leaves, squash blossoms, and lemon juice, then wilt the greens quickly. Remove from the heat and let cool.

2. In a large bowl, combine the feta, ricotta cheese, goat Gouda, lemon zest, the remaining 1 tablespoon olive oil, and the cooled chard mixture. Lightly fold the ingredients together and season with salt and pepper.

3. Position a rack in the top third of the oven and place a sheet pan on the rack. Preheat the oven to 425°F. Lightly brush a 9-inch springform cake pan with oil.

4. Lay 1 sheet of phyllo pastry on a clean work surface. Brush with melted butter and place a second sheet on top, smoothing with the palm of your hand. With a long side facing you, spread just under one-third of the filling in a thin line, 1 inch from the bottom of the phyllo. Brush the uncovered pastry with a little more butter, fold it over the squash mixture, tucking in the filling, then roll the pastry to create a thin sausage. Brush the pastry with butter again, coil into a tight spiral, and lift it into the center of the springform pan.

5. Repeat this process twice more, each time adding to the spiral in the springform. If there is space in the pan at the end, fill the final sheet of phyllo with any remaining squash mixture, roll, and squeeze into the pan.

6. Brush the pie with the egg wash. Place the springform on the hot sheet pan and bake at the top of the oven until the pastry is golden and crisp, about 30 minutes.

7. Let the borek cool for 5 to 10 minutes before removing it from the pan. Slice into wedges like a cake.

Anchovy Salsa Macha

Makes about 3 cups

This spicy anchovy and nut salsa is perfect for adding a kick to any dish. Serve it with grilled meats or vegetables, or use it as a dipping sauce for bread or crackers. This recipe can be easily halved.

1½ cups grapeseed oil or another neutral oil

8 garlic cloves, sliced

½ cup dried anchovies

15 chiles de árbol, stemmed and seeded

2 chiles moritas, stemmed and seeded

½ cup peanuts

2 tablespoons sunflower seeds

1 tablespoon sesame seeds

1 tablespoon pumpkin seeds

1 tablespoon distilled white vinegar, plus more to taste

1 teaspoon fish sauce

Kosher or sea salt

1. In an deep pan, heat ¾ cup of the grapeseed oil over medium heat. Add the sliced garlic and cook gently until the garlic starts to turn golden, about 3 minutes. Add the anchovies and lightly fry them with the garlic until both are golden. Scrape the anchovies, garlic, and cooking oil into a bowl and set aside to cool.

2. Add the remaining ¾ cup oil to the pan and lightly fry the chiles, being careful not to burn them. Scrape the chiles and cooking oil into a bowl and set aside to cool.

3. Wipe out the pan and dry-roast the peanuts, sunflower seeds, sesame seeds, and pumpkin seeds until they are deep golden brown. (Alternatively, you can toast them in the oven.)

4. In a food processor, blend the chiles and reserved oil until smooth. Add the roasted nuts and seeds, vinegar, and fish sauce and pulse until the nuts are chunky.

5. Remove from the food processor and fold in the anchovy/garlic mixture with the oil. Season with salt to taste and add more vinegar if needed to brighten the flavors.

Make Ahead: Store in an airtight container in the refrigerator for up to 1 week.

Stuffed Squid with Chorizo & Hibiscus

Serves 4 to 6

Inspired by the markets of Spain, this dish combines the richness of chorizo with the tangy sweetness of hibiscus—it's a nod to the delicious flavors I grew up with. Squid—which is like shrimp in how easy it is to cook—acts as the casing for the stuffing.

1 cup dried hibiscus (roselles)

3 tablespoons olive oil, plus more for brushing

½ cup finely diced white onion

6 garlic cloves

1 pound fresh Mexican chorizo, casings removed

½ cup cooked long-grain rice

Grated zest of 1 large orange

2 tablespoons orange juice, plus more for serving

Kosher salt

1½ teaspoons smoked paprika

1 teaspoon sweet paprika, plus more for garnish

12 medium squid, cleaned and tentacles removed

1. In a medium saucepan, bring the hibiscus and 2 cups water to a boil over medium-high heat and boil until the roselles are soft, about 15 minutes. Set a sieve over a bowl and pour the hibiscus and cooking liquid into it. Reserve the hibiscus and hibiscus water separately. Once cooled, chop up the hibiscus.

2. In a pan, heat 1 tablespoon of the olive oil over medium heat. Add the onion and sweat for 2 minutes. Microplane 3 of the garlic cloves into the pan and sweat with the onion until fragrant and the onion is translucent, about another 2 minutes.

3. Add the chorizo, cooked rice, two-thirds of the chopped hibiscus, half of the orange zest, and the orange juice. Stir together and add 2 tablespoons of the hibiscus water. Season with salt and cook down until the liquid evaporates. Remove from the heat and let cool.

4. Chop the remaining 3 garlic cloves. In a medium pan, heat the remaining 2 tablespoons olive oil over medium heat. Add the chopped garlic and cook until the garlic is golden brown, about 3 minutes. Add the smoked paprika, sweet paprika, and the remaining chopped hibiscus. Remove from the heat and add 2 tablespoons of the hibiscus water, stirring well. Once cooled, season with salt and mix in the remaining orange zest.

5. Stuff each squid with the chorizo mixture, leaving a little space at the opening of the squid tube. Brush the stuffed squid lightly with olive oil.

6. To avoid overcooking, grill the squid over an open grill at a medium-hot spot, skewering them for easier handling if desired. Higher heat allows for less cook time, which gives you char and color without overcooking. You generally can tell the squid is done cooking when it's no longer slippery.

7. Remove the squid from the grill and place it on a plate. Garnish with more sweet paprika, the hibiscus oil you made in step 4, and a fresh squeeze of orange juice over the top. Serve with the hibiscus sauce on the side.

Chilled Chileatole Corn Soup

Serves 8 to 10

This is the perfect chilled soup that—to me—is the embodiment of summer. Fresh seasonal summer corn creates the base, but ripe summer peppers create the depth. Feel free to play around with whatever peppers appeal to you at your local market. You can easily transform this into a hearty meal in its own right by adding crab, chicken, or vegan cashew crema.

1 poblano pepper, seeded

1 cup greens of choice, such as spinach

1 cup fresh corn kernels

2 jalapeño peppers, seeded

½ cup fresh cilantro

½ bunch of epazote

6 cups vegetable or chicken stock

¼ cup masa dough

Kosher salt

3 ears corn, shucked

½ cup fresh lime juice

½ cup Cotija cheese, grated

1 tablespoon sumac

1 tablespoon Aleppo pepper

Lime wedges, for squeezing

1. In a blender, combine the poblano, greens, fresh corn kernels, jalapeños, cilantro, epazote, and 1½ cups water. Blend on high speed until smooth. Transfer the puree to a large pot and bring to a simmer over medium-low heat.

2. In the same blender, combine the stock and masa dough, blending on high speed until smooth. Add the masa mixture to the pot with the pepper puree and mix well until fully incorporated. Bring the pot back to a simmer and cook for a few minutes so all the flavors mix well but stay green. Season to taste with salt. Remove from the heat and cool in the refrigerator for at least 2 hours.

3. On a cast-iron grill pan or open-fire grill, char the ears of corn until they're nicely cooked with heavy grill marks. Remove from the heat and let cool. With a sharp knife, cut the kernels off the grilled corn and set aside.

4. Remove the soup from the refrigerator and stir in the lime juice. Check for seasoning and adjust as needed. Add the grilled corn kernels.

5. Serve the soup in bowls. Garnish each bowl with Cotija cheese, sumac, Aleppo pepper, and a lime wedge.

   Make Ahead: To make the soup ahead of time, stop at the end of step 2 and store in an airtight container in the refrigerator for up to 1 week or in the freezer for up to 3 months.

Marinated Oysters with Celery & Leek Agrodolce

Serves 4

Skip the played-out shallot vinaigrette that's always accompanying oysters and make this green, earthy and tart agrodolce instead. While oysters are beautiful in their own right, I love to play into their salty brine with equally complex flavors. Plus, preparing oysters at home is something you'll only ever do when having guests over, so enjoy it.

½ cup roughly chopped celery

½ cup roughly chopped leeks

1 cup champagne vinegar

1½ teaspoons sugar

1 teaspoon salt

1 teaspoon mustard seeds

1 bay leaf

1 sprig fresh tarragon

2 dozen oysters of your choice

½ cup olive oil

Toasted crusty bread

Tarragon or other fresh herbs, for garnish

1. In a small heatproof bowl, combine the celery and leeks.

2. In a small pot, combine the vinegar, ½ cup water, the sugar, salt, mustard seeds, bay leaf, and tarragon. Bring to a boil over high heat, stirring occasionally, until the sugar dissolves and the mixture becomes very fragrant.

3. Pour the mixture over the celery and leeks. Allow it to sit until it reaches room temperature. This will brighten the colors and marry the flavors, but the celery and leeks will remain crunchy. Once cooled, refrigerate the bowl of agrodolce for at least 2 hours and up to 2 days in advance.

4. Shuck the oysters, reserving all of the liquor, and place them in a separate bowl. Add the chilled celery and leek agrodolce to the oysters and stir in the olive oil. Marinate in the refrigerator for at least 20 minutes.

5. Remove from the refrigerator and serve the oysters with toasted crusty bread. Garnish with more tarragon or other fresh herbs, if desired.

Skirt Steak with Harissa Brown Butter & Buckwheat

Serves 4

Skirt steak is a great protein option when you're feeding a lot of people or, as is often my case, you're not entirely sure exactly how many people you're feeding. It's a cost-effective cut that's best served thinly sliced, which takes you away from the ounce-per-person math that can drive you crazy. This recipe prepares the steak with a deep, spicy butter sauce and uses buckwheat to facilitate some crunch.

½ pound unsalted butter

½ cup buckwheat groats

Kosher salt

1½ tablespoons harissa

1 tablespoon fresh lemon juice

¼ cup chopped fresh parsley

2 tablespoons olive oil

1 pound skirt steak

½ teaspoon freshly ground black pepper

1. In a medium pan, melt the butter over medium heat until it separates. Add the buckwheat groats and a pinch of salt. Cook the buckwheat groats, stirring, until golden brown and the butter becomes a rich nutty color and flavor, about 5 minutes. Stir in the harissa until incorporated. Remove from the heat and transfer to a bowl.

2. While the mixture is still hot, add the lemon juice. Once it is slightly cooler, finish with the chopped parsley and season with salt, if needed.

3. In a cast-iron grill pan, heat the olive oil over high heat. Season the skirt steak with 1 teaspoon salt and the pepper. Sear each side of the steak, being careful not to overcook, about 3 minutes each side.

4. Remove the steak from the pan and let it rest on a cutting board for 5 minutes. Thinly slice the steak and place it on a serving plate. Drizzle the harissa brown butter and buckwheat over the steak and serve immediately.

Vegan Saffron Rice Pudding

Serves 6 to 8

This saffron rice pudding is a creamy, sweet, and nutty dessert that is perfect for any occasion. Serve it warm or cold and enjoy the rich flavors. I'm a diehard proponent of texture and flavor balance, and this is the perfect dish to make that satisfying combination.

1 cup Arborio rice

One 13.5-ounce can coconut milk

1½ cups oat or rice milk

2 tablespoons sugar

1 teaspoon salt

1 cup golden raisins

1 teaspoon white wine vinegar

Pinch of saffron threads

1 cup hot water

1 cup pistachios, deeply toasted and chopped

1 cup raspberries, crushed

1. In medium nonstick saucepan, combine the rice, coconut milk, oat milk, sugar, and salt. Stir well over medium heat until all the ingredients are thoroughly incorporated.

2. In a bowl, combine the golden raisins, vinegar, saffron threads, and hot water. Stir well and let the mixture sit for a few minutes to allow the saffron to bloom and the raisins to soak up the liquid.

3. Continue to stir the rice mixture over medium heat until it thickens, about 20 minutes. Once the rice is cooked, add the raisin and saffron water mixture and stir until the pudding is smooth and creamy, about 2 minutes. Add more water as needed to achieve a creamy consistency.

4. Serve the pudding garnished with the pistachios and raspberries, allowing the raspberry juice to pool on top.

With a Little Help from My Friends

Learning when to ask for help is one of life's greatest lessons, and that extends to dinner parties. Make your gathering last even longer by inviting a few (trusty) friends over early to join in on the fun and preparations. Enlist your own team of sous-chefs and don't be afraid to let someone surprise you—sometimes it's the least likely person who shows a great interest in learning how to cook . . . and what an honor it is to show them!

How to Play Head Chef

As head chef, people will follow your lead—physically and emotionally. Create a fun kitchen environment with music, drinks, and (the best perk) taste testing. As the leader, you'll want to set the pace with a rewarding timeline.

Easy-to-Pawn-Off Tasks

Chopping
Custom drink making
Setting the table
Plating finished dishes
Stuffing squids
Shucking corn ears
Managing the grill

Souvenirs for Hosting

To me, a trip isn't complete without returning home with some trinkets for my loved ones (and myself). Cities can be explored through so many different lenses, but some of my favorites include chatting up local grocers, sifting through antique stores, or browsing a street market. Don't let luggage space stop you from bringing something home that will spark joy, conversation, and memories of your travels for years to come.

For the Plate

A nice **olive oil** (infused with local ingredients is always a plus)

A jar of **native-to-the-area spices** (I like to include a recipe card to spark creativity)

Cured meat that can survive in your suitcase

Spice blends (even homemade ones, like my go-to: 1 part Aleppo, 1 part sumac, ½ part smoked salt) make for excellent parting gifts at the end of a dinner party.

For the Table

A fun, mismatched, **statement-worthy piece of serveware**

Linens, any and all of them, from a tablecloth to placemats, napkins, or an apron

Tiny glassware for nightcaps

For the Ambiance

Vintage records

Dried flowers

3 DAYS OUT

Invite your friends and get a rough sense of the head count. I personally keep inviting people up until the moment dinner is served, and sometimes even after that. But it never hurts to have an idea of how many people you'll be cooking for.

Grab all the ingredients that are not ones you'll be getting day-of at the farmers' market or fishmonger.

DAY BEFORE DINNER PARTY

Go to the market and get all your fresh ingredients. Once you're home, "process" them to make the following day as easy as possible. Wash greens and store them in water. Make your flower arrangements. Store the cantaloupe in a paper bag with a banana if it needs to ripen a bit more.

Prep your squid and borek fillings.

Make the Agua Fresca.

Prep any and all toppings.

Put your phyllo dough in the refrigerator to soften.

Make sure you have one or two trusted friends available earlier in the day to help you cook everything.

 ### DINNER PARTY!

Go ahead and knock the soup, rice pudding, and potato salad out in the morning.

Then, prep (but don't cook) the borek and the squid.

Once your friends show up, put them to work with any of the aforementioned tasks.

Remember to remove your steak from the fridge at least an hour before grilling. Salt it well beforehand, too!

Once more folks start to roll in, get the grill going, finish off the borek in the oven, set the cold dishes out, and watch everything come together.

A Reimagined Caribbean Feast

WITH DEVONN FRANCIS

DeVonn Francis is the chef and Founding Director of Yardy World, a culinary studio that specializes in creating immersive food experiences and reimagining Caribbean cuisine. DeVonn is famed for creating meals that are sensual and celebratory, chic and joy-filled. His recipes are designed to give people a sense of home, whatever that may mean to them.

Brooklyn summers have a special place in my heart. Every year, for over twenty years, we would drive up the coast from my Virginia hometown to my grandparents' house in Brooklyn, spending long days and longer nights hanging out in family kitchens and living rooms. My family migrated to East Flatbush and Prospect Lefferts Garden between the early '60s and late '70s with the dream of building a life in America.

STEAL MY PLAYLIST

What they brought with them was the music, history, culture, and foodways of the Caribbean and Jamaica. They also brought block parties full of candor and generosity as the days got long and hot during the summer solstice. Any excuse to entertain was a good excuse. Birthdays, weddings, baby showers, baptisms, and graduation ceremonies were all fair game for celebrating. And there was always food involved.

The Brooklyn summer gatherings of my upbringing have shaped the way I cook and gather to this day. I plan my August with these flavors and ceremonial sensibilities in mind: bright and confident tastes, plating that is showy but unfussy, and colorful table settings that speak to the spirit of island life brought to New York at a time when immigration meant having to pool resources to support one another. My favorite dinner parties have been ones where people from all walks of life feel inspired to get dressed up and be the best version of themselves they choose to be. To me, dinner is just as much about theatrics and playing dress-up as it is about having incredible food and drinks.

This dinner party is my ode to summers with family—chosen and otherwise. When I cook, it comes from a place of intuition. I want my recipes to feel both balanced and expressive, only using necessary ingredients so that you can get to the party instead of getting stuck in the kitchen or by the grill all day. You'll find summer fruit and vegetables alongside quick-to-grill fish and savory, pickley things, too. August reminds me of how delicious produce is at the height of the season. You don't have to do much to make the flavor stand out, which is exactly how I like it. Search for produce that can be a star all on its own, and you're over halfway to a dinner party that your guests will savor with every bite.

Cooking, hosting, and generally grounding my life and work in food has taught me three things:

ONE: FOOD SHOULD BE A PIPELINE TO GET RESOURCES BACK TO THE COMMUNITIES WE CARE ABOUT.

Every time you cook, invest in ingredients that you care about. This means farmers benefit from advocating for what they are growing and cooks benefit from learning about new cultures and new ingredients.

TWO: FOOD SHOULD BE AN IMMERSIVE CULINARY EXPERIENCE.

I love making people feel like they're a part of a ritual—you don't necessarily need a special occasion to celebrate solo or with a group. What matters is feeling like you are an active participant. Good party hosts and organizers know how to make the feeling of belonging last beyond the party itself.

THREE: FOOD IS NOT JUST ENTERTAINING, BUT NOURISHING AND EDUCATIONAL AS WELL.

Health and wellness are key components to everyone's livelihood, and chefs should use their expertise to empower others to make positive decisions around nurturing one's self. Eating is crucial to care. In predominantly Black and Brown communities, it is important that food not only reflect where you come from, but also offer hope that food can enliven our daily lives and enrich our futures. I want everyone to feel empowered by what they find in grocery stores and the meals they make for themselves, and for all of us to have the courage to ask better questions about what practicing wellness mindfully might look like.

Tomato Salad with Coconut Crisp

Serves 6 to 8

Late August is my favorite time for harvesting tomatoes because they are often at their ripest. Adding dollops of mascarpone and a dressing of coconut aminos creates a depth of flavor from fat and briny sweetness. This salad is a go-to because it requires only simple knife work and a brief moment of baking the coconut flakes to golden brownness.

¼ cup coconut flakes

2 garlic cloves, thinly sliced

2 teaspoons coconut aminos

1 tablespoon olive oil, plus more for drizzling

Kosher salt

1 to 2 large heirloom tomatoes

¼ cup mascarpone or whole-milk Greek yogurt

½ teaspoon red pepper flakes

1. Position a rack in the center of the oven and preheat the oven to 350°F. Line a sheet pan with parchment paper.

2. Spread the coconut flakes evenly on the lined pan and bake for 4 minutes. The coconut flakes on the outer edges will brown faster than the flakes in the center. Stir the coconut flakes and bake until evenly golden brown, 2 to 3 minutes. Remove from the oven and set aside.

3. In a bowl, combine the garlic, coconut aminos, olive oil, and salt to taste and whisk together to make a dressing.

4. Slice the tomatoes widthwise into ¼-inch wedges, rounds, or half-moons. Add to the bowl with the dressing and toss until well coated.

5. Pull the tomatoes out of the dressing and arrange on a serving platter like playing cards that have fallen randomly out of your hands, some slightly more covered than others. Dress the tomatoes with dollops of the mascarpone, using the back of a spoon to make divots in the dollops, and then spoon in the dressing so that it resembles a shallow pool. Finish with a drizzle of olive oil, chile flakes, and reserved coconut flakes.

Coconut Is a Gift

Coconut is foundational to Caribbean cooking. Whether it is the base of a stew or the crunch of a topping, coconut appears—and reappears—across the cuisine in endless and exciting ways. While you'll get no argument from me that the flavor is incredibly versatile (and appropriate in almost any dish or setting), part of coconut's prevalence has to do with the many forms you can find it in.

Coconut aminos: Coconut sap and sea salt used as a gluten-free-based flavoring agent in place of soy sauce.

Coconut sugar: A not-too-sweet sweetener to be used as a replacement for traditional cane sugar.

Coconut flour: Use it in place of wheat flour to achieve a sweeter, fattier flavor profile.

Coconut vinegar: Fun fact: Over time, coconut water will sour and become vinegar! Use it to season and make salad dressings.

Coconut jelly: Lends your morning smoothies a nice consistency. Also great alongside ceviche!

Coconut meat: Grate or shave it over your cold dishes and desserts as the finishing touch.

Coconut water: Cook your rice in it to infuse an otherwise bland side with tropical flavor.

Coconut cream: Will work as a substitute for most (but not all!) recipes that require milk.

Coconut shells: Use these as decor on your table. Pro tip: They double as dipping bowls!

Pickled Mango & Green Papaya Salad with Tajín

Serves 6 to 8

Green papaya is slightly harder to find than its ripe counterpart, but worth the search in order to get that hearty vegetable quality to contrast the sweet mango. Applying a pickle brine takes this from what would typically be a sweet dish to something vibrant and savory. Throw in a handful of herbs and Tajín seasoning to complete this easy summer salad.

2 mangoes, cut into large wedges

1 green papaya, peeled, seeded, and cut into large cubes

¼ cup sliced (lengthwise into little crescent moons) white onion

2 teaspoons Tajín

1 tablespoon white wine vinegar

2 tablespoons olive oil

Grated zest and juice of 1 lime

1 teaspoon freshly ground black pepper

1 cup fresh mint leaves

½ cup fresh cilantro leaves

1. In a small bowl, combine the mango, papaya, onion, 1 teaspoon of the Tajín, and the vinegar and toss together. Let marinate for at least 10 minutes.

2. Transfer to a rimmed serving platter and drizzle with the olive oil, lime zest, pepper, and lime juice. Garnish with the mint and cilantro, then finish with the remaining 1 teaspoon Tajín.

Grilled Herring with Fried Scallions & Grapes

Serves 6 to 8

Grilled fish is a quick and beautiful meal for the summer months. It's great on its own, of course, but I like to make it my own with a quickly marinated grape and tomato mixture. It's an easy, unexpected addition to a familiar dish that people try and love. You can swap in your favorite small-to-medium fish if you can't find Atlantic herring at your local fishmonger.

4 whole Atlantic herring (1½ pounds each), head on and cleaned

1 cup grapes, halved

½ tablespoon sherry vinegar

2 tablespoons olive oil

1 cup Green Zebra cherry tomatoes (or any small cherry tomatoes), halved

½ teaspoon five-spice powder

Kosher salt

2 tablespoons grapeseed oil

1 bunch of scallions, thinly sliced on the diagonal

1 teaspoon red pepper flakes

Lemon wedges, for squeezing

1. Pat the herring dry and lay them on top of paper towels. Let the herring come to room temperature while you prepare the remainder of your ingredients. If you are grilling, be sure that the grate or plancha is extremely clean to avoid sticking to the surface.

2. In a small bowl, toss together the grapes, vinegar, 1 tablespoon of the olive oil, the tomatoes, five-spice, and salt to taste until well combined.

3. In a small pan, heat the grapeseed oil over medium-high heat. Add the scallions and cook until crispy, 4 to 6 minutes. Drain and let the scallions cool completely on a paper towel to absorb any excess oil.

4. Preheat a grill or a grill pan to medium-high heat. Coat the herring with the remaining 1 tablespoon olive oil, a pinch of salt, and the red pepper flakes. Grill the fish, turning once, until just opaque, 2 to 3 minutes per side, then transfer to a serving platter.

5. Garnish the herring with the tomato and grape mixture, spooning it over the fish, and finish with the fried scallions. Serve with lemon wedges.

Potato Pudding Steamed in Banana Leaf

Serves 6 to 8

This is a classic Jamaican dessert that is part cake and part pudding in consistency. The variety of root vegetables used to make it speaks to the abundance of the islands and gives your guests a feeling of satisfaction at the end of a meal. If you can't find all the traditional roots listed, you can use a variety of sweet potatoes to get a similar result. Banana leaves can also be difficult to source depending on where you live. Frozen leaves are more readily available and easy to work with once fully thawed in the fridge overnight. You can order them online or try your local Hispanic grocer. Otherwise, parchment is a valid alternative.

Banana leaves
1 cup grated yellow yam
1½ cups grated white sweet potato
1 cup grated coco yam (ñame)
2¼ cups canned coconut milk
2½ cups packed dark brown sugar
3 tablespoons unsalted butter
½ teaspoon kosher salt
2 teaspoons vanilla extract
1 teaspoon grated nutmeg

1. Position a rack in the center of the oven and preheat the oven to 375°F. Line a 9-inch springform pan with banana leaves, leaving enough leaf hanging over the edge to cover the pan once it's filled. Place a baking sheet under the springform pan to catch any batter.

2. In a bowl, combine the yellow yam, sweet potato, coco yam, coconut milk, brown sugar, butter, salt, vanilla, and nutmeg. Working in batches, transfer to a blender and process until the mixture is extremely smooth.

3. Pour into the lined springform pan. Make sure the mixture is spread evenly and free of air bubbles by tapping the springform against the sheet pan before placing it in the oven.

4. Bake until a cake tester comes out dry, about 1 hour. If it's still wet, continue to bake in 5-minute increments.

5. Once baked through, turn on the broiler or increase the oven temperature to 500°F. Broil until the top is crunchy and crisp, 3 to 4 minutes, being careful to not let it burn. You should be able to tap and hear it with the back of a spoon.

6. Remove the pudding from the oven and let cool slightly for easier slicing, then serve.

Jerk Shrimp Skewers

Serves 6 to 8

Most are familiar with the chicken version of jerk, but when this spicy paste is applied to seafood, it makes a world of difference. If you want to make this more intricate, you can pair this grilled shrimp with hunks of chayote to add moments of coolness in between peppery bites.

Jerk Paste

2 bunches of scallions, roughly chopped
2 Scotch bonnet peppers, halved lengthwise
3 garlic cloves
3-inch piece fresh ginger, peeled
   and thinly sliced
2 tablespoons grated orange zest
2 tablespoons ground allspice (pimento)
1 tablespoon light brown sugar
1 tablespoon kosher salt
1 teaspoon freshly cracked black pepper
2 teaspoons fresh thyme leaves
2 teaspoons sweet paprika
¼ teaspoon ground nutmeg
1 tablespoon soy sauce

Shrimp Skewers

1 pound large shrimp, peeled and deveined,
   tails left on
Lime wedges

1. Make the jerk paste: In a food processor, combine the scallions, Scotch bonnets, garlic, ginger, orange zest, allspice, brown sugar, salt, black pepper, thyme, paprika, nutmeg, and soy sauce. Process to a coarse paste, 30 to 45 seconds.

2. For the shrimp skewers: Lay a shrimp belly side down so that it's flat on a clean surface. Insert a skewer through the tail and straight through to the head end Repeat with the remaining shrimp.

3. Place the shrimp skewers down on a clean, medium-hot grill. Immediately baste the shrimp with the jerk sauce, coating all the shrimp before taking them off the grill. Baste with the sauce once more before serving. Dress with a squeeze of lime juice or serve with a side of lime wedges.

Chickpea Fritters in Green Salsa

Serves 6 to 8

Bathing in green sauce and full of warm spice, these fritters are a great way to get the most out of dry chickpeas. They can be served as an appetizer or even a main course with the right accompaniments. The blend of herbs offers a refreshing and zesty balance to the heartiness of the fritter.

Fritters

1 cup dried chickpeas

3 garlic cloves, roughly chopped

2 teaspoons ground turmeric

1 teaspoon ground cumin

1 teaspoon ground coriander

1 teaspoon red pepper flakes

¼ teaspoon ground cinnamon

1 tablespoon fresh thyme leaves

Kosher salt

2 to 4 tablespoons coconut oil

2 fresh bay leaves

Green Salsa

¼ cup cilantro, picked with tender stems

¼ cup parsley, picked with tender stems

¼ cup thinly sliced shallot (cut lengthwise)

1 Scotch bonnet or serrano pepper, finely chopped

¼ cup toasted coconut chips

1 tablespoon raisins, coarsely chopped

1 tablespoon peanuts, toasted and coarsely chopped

2 tablespoons lime juice

¼ cup olive oil

Kosher salt

Lime wedges, for squeezing

1. In a medium bowl, combine the chickpeas with water to cover by at least 3 inches and soak until they triple in volume (this can be set overnight).

2. Measure out three-quarters of the chickpeas and pulse in a food processor until the mixture is coarse. Scrape out of the food processor into a bowl and set aside.

3. Add the remaining one-quarter of the chickpeas to the food processor along with the garlic and process to a loose paste. Add a little bit of water gradually if it takes a while for the chickpeas to form a chunky paste.

4. Combine both chickpea mixes in a bowl. Add the turmeric, cumin, coriander, pepper flakes, cinnamon, thyme, and salt to taste and mix until homogeneous.

5. With a large spoon or ice cream scoop, form fritters into long ovals by scooping and then rolling the mixture into your hands until they resemble a football shape.

6. In a large fry pan, heat the coconut oil and bay leaves over medium heat. Working in batches, fry the chickpea fritters, turning them periodically to achieve an even golden brown color on all sides, 5 to 6 minutes. Once you notice the bay leaves are about to turn golden brown, discard them. As you notice burnt flecks floating in your oil, strain them out with a metal sieve so that you can reuse the oil without the flavor turning bitter. Transfer the fried fritters to a paper towel to drain excess oil. Immediately salt the fritters as they come out of the oil so that the salt is absorbed while they are warm.

7. Make the green salsa: In a bowl, combine the cilantro, parsley, shallot, Scotch bonnet, coconut chips, raisins, peanuts, lime juice, olive oil, and a couple generous pinches of salt and mix thoroughly.

8. Add the green salsa to the bottom of a serving plate and add the fritters on top, finishing with any leftover herbs and a squeeze of lime juice.

Sweet Star Fruit & Salted Cream

Serves 6 to 8

This is a simple dessert that comes together quickly—you simply need to let the fruit absorb the flavors of rum and tamarind in the refrigerator for a short period of time. Star fruit is marinated in rum, tamarind, and sugar to bring out the best qualities of the fruit's flavor while also adding a touch of acidity balanced with dollops of crème fraîche.

1 tablespoon dark or white rum

1 tablespoon tamarind concentrate

2 teaspoons light brown sugar

1 teaspoon ground cinnamon

2 teaspoons coconut vinegar or white wine vinegar

2 star fruit, sliced into ¼-inch-thick stars

1 cup crème fraîche

Flaky sea salt

Grated zest of 1 lime

½ cup fresh mint leaves

1. In small bowl, mix the rum, tamarind concentrate, brown sugar, cinnamon, and vinegar and stir until the sugar crystals are completely dissolved. Add the star fruit and mix gently just until the liquid mixture evenly coats the fruit. Set aside and let macerate for a minimum of 1 hour and up to 24 hours in the refrigerator.

2. When ready to serve, arrange the star fruit and crème fraîche on a plate, alternating layers of star fruit and dollops of crème fraîche. Finish with flaky sea salt, the lime zest, and the mint leaves.

Winter-Killer

Makes 1 cocktail

A take on the classic Painkiller, this creamy and bright beachside cocktail complements a late-summer menu incredibly well. It also adds delicious acidity with the incorporation of passion fruit against the herbal Cardamaro. Cardamaro, if you've never tried it, is a wine-based aperitif infused with cardoon and blessed thistle. It's likened to a more drinkable Cynar, and you might just find you love having it in your liquor cabinet. You can easily make a big batch of this by swapping ounces for cups.

Ice

1 ounce dark rum

1 ounce Cardamaro

4 ounces passion fruit juice

1 ounce pineapple juice

1 ounce cream of coconut

Pineapple peel, for garnish

Grated cardamom, for garnish

1. In an ice-filled cocktail shaker, combine the rum, Cardamaro, passion fruit juice, pineapple juice, and cream of coconut and shake vigorously until frost appears on the sides.

2. Add a piece of pineapple peel to a glass with ice. Strain the cocktail into the glass. Garnish with grated cardamom.

A Distinctly Yardy Tablescape

While I will always advocate for less fuss when it comes to hosting, there is something to be said about an artfully set table. My perfect table is symmetrical yet accidental, organic yet defined by clean lines, and—most important—full of color. A well-set table can be as important as a main course. It's responsible for inviting people to sit down and making them feel welcome, like there is always a place for them at the table.

1 long table

6 to 8 of your closest friends and lovers

6 to 8 napkins, mismatched or otherwise

1 bold, solid linen tablecloth

5 to 6 colorful flower varieties, arranged

Taper candles galore

Equally spaced trivets for family-style serving

Extra serving utensils or tongs

1. Cover your dinner table with the cloth. Don't iron it—it's only going to get ruffled up by the good times anyway.
2. Anchor the table with simple place settings. Big plates, napkins, and cutlery should all be equally spaced around the table, leaving as much room as possible in the middle for food and decor.
3. Situate your floral centerpiece(s) in the middle or anchored on either side of the table. Take a seat in the chair across from the arrangement to ensure that it's short enough to see over. You don't want your guests craning their necks to speak to one another. (See Everyone's a Florist, page 168, for floral arrangement tips.)
4. Assess your dinner menu and plating plans to gain a rough idea of what will go where on the table. Remember, there's nothing wrong with serving something directly from your Always Pan. It's easier, it's fewer dishes, and it keeps food warmer, longer.
5. Fill in negative space with tall taper candles. Ask a friend to light them as you bring out the dishes.
6. Assemble all of your table elements a day or two before your party. Setting a table can be a stimulating creative ritual if you give yourself the time. Doing it ahead of time will only allow you to have more fun with it! Use produce peels, wrapping paper, and rumpled fabric to give your table a "lived in" feel.

Everyone's a Florist

As much as a floral arrangement can turn a regular table into something truly interesting and beautiful, a sad arrangement can do the opposite. It's okay. Flowers are intimidating with their delicate stems and tendency to flop around. With a few (very simple) guiding principles in your arsenal, you'll be able to turn even the most everyday bodega blooms into something special.

The Five Elements of a Successful Flower Arrangement

THE BASE
1 to 2 types of sturdy leafy greens

Palm, sword fern, small monstera leaves

THE STATEMENT
1 larger bloom that fills in negative space

Protea, dahlias, orchids

THE TEXTURE
Something frilly for dimension

Mimosa, acacia, parrot tulip

THE HEIGHT
1 delicate, linear flower for a wild pop

Delphinium, stock, larkspur

THE SURPRISE
An unexpected element to give personality

Kumquat branches, artichoke hearts, tangerines on kebab skewers

On the Down-Low

Keep your arrangement lower than you would expect. This is important for arrangements where people need (and hopefully want!) to talk to one another across the table. Opt for wider, squatter vases to help you achieve this.

Keep It in Place

If you see yourself making more than a few flower arrangements a year, it might be wise to invest in a floral frog. These spikey bases grip flowers in place, making it incredibly easy to play around with different arrangements. If you don't want to go the floral frog route, simply create a grid of tape across the top of your vase to help keep everything where you want it. And if you're being really scrappy, just use a rubber band for the center portion of the arrangement, and fill in the outside perimeter with extra greens to cover any patches.

AT THE BEGINNING OF A NEW SEASON

I start by making a playlist and slowly add to it week by week. This comes in handy for all of the dinner parties I hold in one season and is also something you can send to guests to remember the time you spent together.

14 DAYS OUT

Send a save the date for any party under 12 to 14 people. (Anything bigger than that, allow for 3 to 4 weeks.)

6 DAYS OUT

Make sure all your linens and laundry are cleaned. I have dinner parties pretty frequently, so my laundry person sees me fairly often. It's always the last thing that I remember to do, but I've gotten in the habit of setting calendar reminders for things that need to be cleaned ahead of time that I can't get to myself.

3 DAYS OUT

This is when I do the bulk of my shopping for specialty ingredients. If my ingredients are coming from far away, I'll allow an extra 2 to 3 days because they're being flown from the Caribbean. I like to break my shopping days down into a 2- to 3-day process so that when I wake up I can jump right into cooking and mise-ing dishes that take a bit more time.

2 DAYS OUT

Shop for delicate greens and fresh vegetables that you want to be pristine the next day.

1 DAY OUT

The day before the party, I'm thinking about what I'm going to wear and most likely getting a mani/pedi! Beyond just taking care of your guests, it's really important for you to take care of yourself. When you feel good, that energy comes across to your guests. How you take care of yourself should be just as important as how you take care of your dinner party guests.

Send reminders to your guests! As much as I know my friends love my food, I also know that last-minute cancellations (or plus-ones) are inevitable.

DINNER PARTY!

You're going to sometimes have to take a deep breath and realize that no matter how much you plan, some things are susceptible to change. That's totally okay! Take note of all the work you've done and be proud that you've gotten this far in your planning process. No great host became that way overnight.

A (Re)Birthday Party

WITH SUSAN KIM

Susan Kim is the founder of Doshi, a traveling food pop-up inspired by Korean home cooking. Despite Susan's classical culinary training (from the likes of Chez Panisse), her approach is untraditional and unfussy, which ultimately results in dishes that will have you redefining what you consider to be authentic.

STEAL
MY
PLAYLIST

While I almost always host this dinner party at my home in Brooklyn, I am writing this half a world away in Seoul. I was born here, but I don't have many memories from when I lived in Korea. The ones I do have are all related to food. Now that I think about it, that means that my earliest memories . . . *ever* . . . are about food. I guess it should come as no surprise, then, that I grew up to dedicate much of my life, work, and time to food.

While my cooking career has taken me all the way from the kitchens of Chez Panisse to starting an international pop-up called Doshi, I still find cooking at home for those I am closest with to be one of my favorite cooking (and eating) experiences.

I think about seasons not only in terms of produce and weather, but also as personal resets. For example, I try to get a Korean scrub every season. If you've ever been splayed out on one of those plastic-lined massage tables, you know this intensive exfoliating session is a physical reset in the most literal sense. Throwing a dinner party is another catalyst for seasonal resets, and one I highly recommend. September has come to be the month I most reliably host for a lot of reasons, one of which is that it's my birth month. (Happy birthday to me!)

September always feels like a giant resetting of the clock—a rebirth of sorts. When I was growing up, my birthday coincided with the beginning of the school year, which inevitably symbolized the end of an era (the era being summer break). Translation: I was about to spend a lot less time at my southern Californian apartment complex's pool. As I am sure many can relate, this moment of change wasn't all bad. It was, after all, a new beginning—both in age and school grade—which ultimately left me feeling hopeful and full of promise. While I now have years separating me from the end-of-summer, school-is-starting jitters, this time of year always brings back old feelings of hopeful anticipation and resetting. It's like my own personal New Year. A happy side effect of these nostalgic feelings is that it inspires me to cook *really good* celebratory-yet-healing food for my close friends and family.

Along with *really good* food, the secret to any dinner party . . . or life, for that matter . . . is to *vibe check*. Don't hate me; this phrase is the closest thing I have found in English for the Korean concept of *bun-wigi* (ambiance), and *nunchi* (reading the room). Nunchi is super important when hosting a dinner party. No matter how much you've organized and planned ahead, certain things (and dishes!) won't play out exactly as you envisioned—and that's okay. Home cooking is at its best when it's intuitive and instinctual—substituting ingredients thoughtfully, making use of what you already have in your pantry or fridge. The same philosophies can and should be applied to your hosting.

You can't control most things in life, but you can attempt to set the vibe, the bun-wigi. Your guests (friends!) are looking to you for your reaction. Advice I wholeheartedly agree with from Julia Child is to *never* talk about how bad the food is. Don't self-deprecate. Don't get hung up on the overcooked piece of steak. A dinner party, like a metaphor for life in general, is the result and the summation of many parts, and it's probably not that bad!

Put your guests to work, or not! Okay, so some of my friends need to be kept busy, even as guests. Everyone deals with social anxiety in different ways and some people like the distraction of having something to do. Give them a task in the kitchen, or ask for help setting the table. Use your intuition to make sure everyone feels welcome at your table. That is both the honor and responsibility of hosting. After all, food is both healing and celebratory, and I think dinner parties can be the same.

Birthday Soup aka Seaweed Soup

Serves 4 to 6

Birthday soup is seaweed soup for Koreans: Miyeok-guk. It's given to new mothers in the hospital because there's a strong belief in the nutritional healing powers of seaweed. When I was growing up, my mom made it for me every birthday. The seaweed she used would be a mix of silky, slurpy, delicate strands mixed with thicker, tougher, chewier pieces . . . I think it's a metaphor for our people!

One 6-inch piece kombu

1 cup dried shiitake mushrooms

3 to 4 pieces dried fatty anchovies

1 pound Manila clams or cockles (or both!)

2 tablespoons fish sauce

2 tablespoons soy sauce

1 jalapeño pepper, thinly sliced

½ cup fresh wakame seaweed

1 tray sea urchin (optional)

A note on sourcing: This recipe (as do others in my chapter) presents a great opportunity to go to your local Asian grocer. While ingredients like wakame seaweed and sea urchin are available at, say, a Whole Foods these days, you'll be able to source more of what you need at H Mart.

1. In a pot, make the dashi stock by combining the kombu, shiitakes, dried anchovies, and 8 cups water. Bring to a boil, then reduce the heat and let simmer for 30 minutes. Remove from the heat and let cool down. Strain the anchovy broth and discard the solids.

2. Wash the clams and place them in a large bowl. Cover them with cold water, then rinse and agitate the clams—really shake it up. Repeat this process with clean cold water until no visible amount of sand is at the bottom of the bowl. Keep the cleaned clams in the refrigerator until ready to cook.

3. In a pot, bring 6 cups of the anchovy broth to a boil. Season the broth with 1 tablespoon of the fish sauce and 1 tablespoon of the soy sauce. Add the sliced jalapeño and clams, reduce the heat to a simmer, cover, and cook for 1 minute. Lift the lid to check. The soup is ready when all the clams have opened, about 5 minutes. Discard any clams that have not opened.

4. Add the wakame seaweed. Ladle the soup into bowls. Drape a few pieces of sea urchin onto each bowl, if using.

Gingery Geotjeori, a Fresh Kimchi

Serves 6 to 8

Kimchi is basically synonymous with fermentation, and it's arguably the globe's most recognizable fermented product. But geotjeori is less well known; it's a fresh-style kimchi, with minimum fermenting or aging, best enjoyed immediately as a refreshing, crunchy, almost-salad. If it's not eaten immediately all at once (one head of napa cabbage yields quite a bit), it will continue to ferment. The cabbage you enjoy on day one will not taste the same as day three, and that's the fun of it. The longer it continues to age (i.e., ferment), the more gifts (i.e., flavor) it will yield. The depths and nuanced umami layers of the kimchi will continue to develop. Make a kimchi stew with pork belly or fried rice (kimchi and butter together, yes!).

1 head napa cabbage

2 tablespoons kosher salt

4 ounces fresh ginger

½ cup grapeseed or other neutral oil

3 tablespoons gochugaru (Korean chile flakes)

6 garlic cloves, Microplaned

2 tablespoons fish sauce

1 bunch of scallions, thinly sliced

1 pound daikon, grated

1. Quarter the head of cabbage lengthwise, cutting through the core. Rinse out any visible dirt under cold water. Remove the core from each quartered cabbage piece and slice the cabbage crosswise into 1-inch pieces. Season with the salt.

2. Peel the ginger and slice it into 1-inch-long matchsticks.

3. In a nonstick pan, heat the oil over medium heat. Add the ginger pieces and sizzle until golden brown, about 3 minutes.

4. Scrape the ginger and all the oil from the pan into a large bowl. Add the gochugaru, garlic, fish sauce, scallions, and daikon. With a rubber spatula, mix and bring the paste together in the bowl.

5. Add the cabbage to the bowl, leaving behind any water collected at the bottom. Mix the cabbage in the paste thoroughly, making sure all the leaves are evenly coated.

6. You can enjoy immediately or store in an airtight container in the fridge for up to 1 week.

Namul (Korean Cooked Greens)

Serves 4 to 6

"Namul" is a term I associate with cooked greens. Traditionally, it's made with dehydrated vegetables and roots. (Dehydration was a key preservation method—along with fermentation—to get through the long Korean winters.) I know I crave it when my body needs it.

1 head of Tuscan kale

1 bunch of rainbow or ruby chard

2 tablespoons olive oil

1 tablespoon yuzu koshō

1 tablespoon soy sauce

1 teaspoon kosher salt, plus more to taste

1. Bring a large pot of water to a boil.

2. Strip the kale from the stems and midribs and separate the leaves. Do the same with the chard. Dice up the stems and midribs. Add the kale leaves to the boiling water and cook until tender, about 3 minutes. Remove the kale with a spider strainer. Repeat the process with the chard leaves. Add the kale stems, midribs, and chard stems and cook until tender, about 6 minutes (note: kale stems will take longer than the chard stems).

3. To cool the greens and stems down, spread them out on a sheet pan. After they are cool enough to handle, chop up the leaves into 1-inch pieces. Taking a handful of leaves at a time, wring out as much water as possible.

4. In a large bowl, mix greens with the olive oil, yuzu koshō, soy sauce, and salt. Season with more salt to taste.

Chestnut Rice

Serves 6 to 8

"Have you eaten?" *That's the greeting I hear when I enter the door to my parents' place. More specifically:* "Have you eaten rice?" *The word* bap *translates literally to "rice," but it's also a catch-all to mean the meal. All the other dishes happen around the rice. One must have rice for the Korean table—it's called* bap sang *(the set table) for a reason. This particular version feels autumnal and luxurious. I love fresh chestnuts and ginkgo nuts, but both items have a very small season of availability. Good news: If you can't find them or they're out of season, there are vacuum-packed offerings of both items in the frozen section of your local Asian grocery store. If you have an impulse to season the rice, please don't. The rice serves as a crucial canvas, the foundation, the center that holds everything together. It will get seasoned as the meal progresses with the braising liquid from* Galbi Jjim aka Braised Short Ribs *(page 180), the kimchi juices, and so on.*

3 cups short-grain white rice
1 cup short-grain sweet (glutinous) white rice
1 pound frozen peeled chestnuts
2 tablespoons frozen ginkgo nuts

1. In a large bowl, rinse both rices with cold water until the water looks clear (filling and dumping the water about three times).

2. In a pot, combine the rinsed rice with 8 cups fresh water and bring to a boil over high heat. Reduce heat to the lowest setting possible. Add the chestnuts and ginkgo nuts, cover, and simmer for 20 minutes. Remove from the heat but keep the lid on and let it steam for 10 minutes on residual heat.

3. Remove the lid. With a rice paddle or spoon, fluff up the rice, mixing in the chestnuts and gingko nuts.

Galbi Jjim aka Braised Short Ribs

Serves 4 to 6

Galbi jjim was almost always served on special occasions when I was growing up—it's a celebratory dish. Like most braises, this will only get better with time, so if you have the bandwidth to braise it the day before your dinner party, it'll get that overnight alchemy that happens in the fridge. If you're able to make this ahead of time, simply let it cool on the stovetop before storing it covered in the refrigerator. To bring it back to serving temperature, reheat it low and slow on the stovetop, giving it a good stir to reintegrate any ingredients that have separated. The process this recipe calls for is really great for any tough cut of meat. The whole point is to bring a tough cut to a very tender place. Feel free to experiment with other tough meats like oxtail, for example. As always, don't be afraid to talk to your butcher about substitutions if you're ever interested in trying something different.

3 pounds bone-in short ribs, cut into 1½-inch cubes

¼ cup kosher salt (preferably a low-salinity salt, such as Diamond Crystal)

Freshly ground black pepper

2 cups soy sauce

½ cup mirin

½ cup maple syrup

½ cup rice vinegar

3 tablespoons olive oil

1 pound yellow onions, halved and thinly sliced

4 ounces fresh ginger, peeled and thinly sliced

6 garlic cloves, grated

1 pound daikon, peeled, halved lengthwise, and cut into ½-inch chunks

½ pound carrots, peeled and cut into ½-inch chunks

½ pound Yukon Gold potatoes, peeled and cut into ½-inch chunks

6-inch piece fresh horseradish root, peeled and Microplaned, for garnish

1 bunch of perilla leaves, torn, for garnish

1. Season the short ribs with the salt and pepper. If possible, do this the night before and store covered in the fridge overnight. Seasoning ahead of time allows the salt to do its job of making the meat more tender and flavorful.

2. In a bowl, combine the soy sauce, 2 cups water, the mirin, maple syrup, and vinegar. Set the braising liquid aside.

3. In a pot or Dutch oven, heat the oil over medium heat. Add the onions, ginger, and garlic and cook together for about 2 minutes. Light browning is okay.

4. Pour the braising liquid into the pot. Add the seasoned short rib pieces, then place the daikon, carrots, and potatoes on top of the short ribs. Cover the pot and bring to a boil. Once it's boiling, reduce the heat to a simmer and braise until the ribs are fork-tender and practically falling off the bone, about 2 hours.

5. Serve with the potatoes and carrots, some of the remaining braising liquids, the grated horseradish, and torn perilla leaves.

Make Ahead: You can make the entire recipe 2 to 3 days before your dinner party. Once the pot or Dutch oven you used for the braise is fully cooled, cover it with the lid and store it as is in the refrigerator. To reheat, bring to a low simmer over medium heat on the stovetop.

Tian of Eggplant, Summer Squash, Tomato, Basil & Perilla

Serves 4 to 6

This layered vegetable dish reminds me of the ratatouille shown in the food critic's memory in the movie Ratatouille. *It's definitely a labor of love. With shingled layers, it's a beautiful dish to present at the dinner table and showcases the beauty of the long summer season. It can also be served at room temperature, so you can make this entire dish a day ahead of time to make your hosting day that much less stressful.*

1 pound eggplant, cut crosswise into slices ¼ inch thick

1 pound summer squash, cut crosswise into slices ¼ inch thick

1 pound tomatoes, cut crosswise into slices ¼ inch thick

Kosher salt

1 cup olive oil

1 bunch of basil, leaves picked and torn

1 bunch of perilla leaves, torn

1. Preheat the oven to 400°F.

2. Season the eggplant, squash, and tomatoes with salt.

3. Oil a medium pan liberally, with about ½ cup of the oil. Begin arranging the vegetables. The idea is to shingle them in layers, like a gratin. The vegetables should be tightly packed in. Drizzle the remaining olive oil on top, then tuck the herbs in between the layers sporadically, reserving some for garnish. Cover the pan with foil.

4. Bake for 20 minutes. Uncover and reduce the oven temperature to 350°F. Continue to bake the tian for another 45 minutes, checking periodically and pressing down with a spatula.

5. Garnish with the remaining basil and perilla leaves.

Chopped Liver

Serves 4 to 6

If birthdays are good for one thing, it's having all your favorite foods on the table at once, regardless of whether they "make sense" together. Enter: chopped liver, a longtime favorite of mine that really spoke to me when I first tried it. This traditional Jewish dish is great to have out and ready when your guests arrive. I like to serve it with roughly broken up bits of matzo for a spread-like situation that is ideal for that initial grazing hour when everyone slowly trickles in.

Neutral oil
1 pound chicken livers, cleaned
2 tablespoons sherry vinegar
4 shallots, diced
6 eggs, hard-boiled and peeled
1 cup fresh parsley leaves, chopped
Kosher salt and freshly ground black pepper
Matzo, broken into pieces, for serving

1. In a pan, heat a couple tablespoons of neutral oil over medium-high heat until it shimmers. Add the chicken livers and sear evenly on all sides, cooking until only the last traces of pink remain on the inside, about 6 minutes. Remove from the heat and transfer the livers to a large bowl to cool.

2. Deglaze the pan with the sherry vinegar, scraping any of the chicken liver debris with a spatula or wooden spoon. Pour the liquid over the cooked chicken livers, making sure you get all the bits from the bottom of the pan. Let cool.

3. In the same pan, heat a couple tablespoons of neutral oil over medium heat. Add the shallots and cook until translucent, about 3 minutes—you do not want a bunch of color.

4. In a food processor, combine the cooled-down chicken livers and liquids along with the shallots. Pulse until integrated but the texture is still slightly coarse and not fully pureed.

5. Scrape out of the food processor into a large bowl. Chop up the hard-boiled eggs and add them to the bowl along with the parsley. Fold them in to incorporate and season to taste with salt and pepper.

6. Serve in a shallow bowl with broken matzo pieces and a butter or cheese knife for spreading.

Late-Summer Tomato Tonnato

Serves 4 to 6

This was a dish conceptualized by one of my significant, defining loves. He was an incredible cook, especially with Italian cuisine. We both loved vitello tonnato, a dish that is typically served cold, featuring thin pieces of meat alongside a tuna-based emulsion. In place of the traditional veal, this recipe uses katsuobushi (bonito flakes), which keeps everything appropriately tuna- and Susan-themed. Please note that consuming raw eggs can increase your risk of foodborne illness, so I strongly recommend you use fresh, pasteurized eggs when making the mayo.

4 large eggs, separated

1½ cups olive oil

1 teaspoon kosher salt, plus more to taste

2 tablespoons grated lemon zest

2 tablespoons fresh lemon juice

8 ounces tinned or jarred tuna in oil, drained

2 pounds heirloom tomatoes,
  cut into thick rounds

Freshly ground black pepper

½ cup pitted Castelvetrano olives

1 cup katsuobushi, for garnish

1. In a food processor, blend the egg yolks and start to slowly drizzle in the olive oil while keeping the processor running on the lowest setting, until it is fully incorporated and thickened into a mayonnaise-like consistency. You can also do this by hand with a whisk, but blending is much easier.

2. Add the salt, lemon zest, lemon juice, and tuna. Process in the food processor until everything is incorporated.

3. Spoon the tuna sauce onto the bottom of a plate. Arrange the tomato slices on top of the sauce, and season them with salt and pepper. Scatter the olives over and garnish with the katsuobushi.

Anything Can Be Banchan

In the Kim household, anything can be banchan in the right context. Minced garlic. Olives. Sliced-up Kraft singles. Setting out banchan can be, at the very least, an incredibly effective way to clean out the refrigerator and at its most a grand, albeit tiny-scaled, way of presenting the fruits of your labor. The Namul (page 178) and Gingery Geotjeori (page 176), for example, find a natural home as banchan, but not everything has to be made at home. Banchan is a great format for showing off your latest H Mart haul, giving a second life to the jar of kosher pickles that has been hanging out since your last sandwich phase, or presenting condiments in a chicer-than-usual way. Use banchan as your opportunity to add some customization options for your guests. Encourage playing with flavors. Try an unsuspecting combination. There are endless possibilities you can present, but I do try to create a bit of balance in the form of . . .

Something Fermented
Seasoned sesame leaves

Something Tart
Seasoned pickled radish

Something Surprising
Cuttlefish

Something Spicy
Young radish

Something Crunchy
Stir-fried black beans

FLATTERING LIGHTING FOR YOU & YOUR GUESTS

I've often said the key to life is great lighting—when done right, everyone looks good. As a longtime host, I've picked up a few tricks over the years. My biggest takeaway? Have many different sources all over the place. This gives you the luxury of customization. While overhead, *I-could-do-surgery-in-this-light* has a utility when you're cooking, warm, soft, indirect light is much preferable when you're eating. I personally rely heavily on candlelight. If lighting a bunch of candles while you have guests over freaks you out (I get it!), try casting your existing lamps and overheads in a new light . . . literally. Take your bedside lamp and place it on the floor in a corner. Angle your desk lamp up and away from the table. Cover your floor lamp with a scarf to add warmth. Turn on a bedroom light down the hall and crack the door. Trust me, once you start noticing lighting and all its particulars, you won't be able to stop curating your environment.

SOURCES OF LIGHT

Beeswax candles
Warm-hued bulbs
Vintage lamps

Scarves on lampshades
iPhone light
Table lamp on the floor

Over-the-oven light
Bedroom light

6 DAYS OUT

Send out the vibe check to see if your group is free for a dinner party.

4 DAYS OUT

Go to the butcher to get the short ribs.

3 DAYS OUT

Salt and pepper the short ribs.

2 DAYS OUT

Go shopping for ingredients. First go to your local Asian grocer for premade things to put on your banchan (see Anything Can Be Banchan, opposite), ingredients you may or may not need to source, like gochugaru, ginkgo nuts, kombu, etcetera.

Go ahead and braise the short ribs! Keep them in the pot and refrigerate once fully cooled.

1 DAY OUT

Get prepped the day ahead (if that suits you!). All these recipes are just as good or better made the day before: Tian, Namul, Tonnato, dashi stock for the Birthday Soup, and Chopped Liver.

DINNER PARTY!

Make the Birthday Soup with your prepared dashi stock.

Do something that makes you feel good: Take a shower, make a playlist, go on a walk.

Make the Chestnut Rice.

Chop the vegetables and garnishes.

Plate the banchan.

Reheat the short ribs.

Make any recipes you didn't make the day before.

Spooky Stoops & Frightening Feasts

WITH ANGEL DIMAYUGA

Chef and transdisciplinary artist Angel doesn't do anything halfway. They have a remarkable ability to make the extravagant feel achievable, or to make the achievable feel extravagant. Their many accomplishments include, but are not limited to, being the Food & Culture Creative Director at Standard Hotels and coauthoring *Filipinx: Heritage Recipes from the Diaspora.*

STEAL MY PLAYLIST

One thing that has remained absolutely steadfast since my childhood: October is my favorite month of the year. I have several, completely unbiased reasons for this. I am an October Libra, it's Filipino American History Month, National Coming Out Day, and—perhaps my ultimate reason and the inspiration for this month's dinner party—Halloween.

Yes, I am a chef, but that's not all. I am also an artist, organizer, and community advocate, which has taken many shapes over the years, but the important thing to note here is that I've gotten really good at throwing parties. And dressing for them. (Again, I am an October Libra, so "outfit" and "costume" might as well be synonyms in my book.) This is not going to be your typical sit-down dinner party. It's a two-part choreography, an afternoon neighborhood hang that bleeds seamlessly into an intimate evening, an activity-forward feast for kids (or the kid inside us all) followed by a lazy, boozy dinner to wind down. Inspired by my childhood, when the line between Halloween and birthday was blurred beyond recognition, this dinner party is a celebration of all things October, whatever that may be for you.

PART ONE: SPOOKY STOOPS

The first part of this gathering starts in the afternoon, when the sun is still high enough to warm the chilly air. To paint a picture for you: I host this party on my Brooklyn stoop rather than a backyard because I want this half of the party to feel connected to the neighborhood and bring the community together. The setup is simple: Fill a table with spooky drinks, monster-themed cookies, and homemade candies, and you're almost good to go . . .

The main attraction is the pabitin. Much akin to the piñata, pabitin is a traditional Filipino game that yields instant gratification in the form of candy and small toy prizes. The goodies are hung from a wooden grid that is hoisted up and down by an adult (or two), encouraging the players to jump and claim their rewards. The players in question? Any little ones you know, and, in the spirit of trick or treating, any kids who walk by and look on with amazement (trust me, they will). If you and your crew are more of the fur-babies variety, there's also a canine version you can play.

PART TWO: WIND-DOWN DINNER

Once the sun is set and the treats are won, it's time to invite your friends who don't have strict bedtimes inside for an already-prepared dinner designed with cozy closeness in mind. I am lucky to have a working fireplace, which will be prepped and ready with the strike of a match. If you don't have a fireplace, that's okay. Achieve fireplace-level coziness however you know how. It's just what the month (and this party) demand.

The secret to this meal is that it requires hardly any moment-of or just-before preparation and cooking, meaning you can be super present at both parts one and two of the party. Have a bitter batched cocktail already made and waiting for you. The curry will be covered, some rice will be hanging out on the always convenient "keep warm" setting, and fresh veggies will balance out the sugar overload we couldn't help but partake of earlier. With no doorbell interruptions, a meal fully prepped out in advance, and a promise to do the dishes in the morning, you get the chance to properly relax at your own dinner party. We'll warm our toes in front of the fire, chill in a cuddle puddle, and giggle while we reflect on another successful, wacky-fun October we had together, all the while sipping a nice drink and refilling our nourishing bowls 'til we're sleepy.

Use this chapter like a buffet—scale and take what you wish. Share the prep with friends. No stoop? Party on the sidewalk or make it an intimate party in your yard. Shift the timing to earlier in the day. Substitute with takeout or delivery. Have a friend pick up candy. Use the chapter any time of the year: Pabitin is popular for birthdays, and wind-down dishes are good for a weeknight meal. Most important: Successful entertaining hinges on you, the host, feeling playful and having fun, so cut your stressors wherever they arise. The best barometer for knowing whether your guests are having fun is to ask yourself if you are!

Build Your Own Potion Station

What is a spooky stoop hang without a science lab/witch lair–themed drink bar? The key to making a potion station is to make it simple, but full of options so that people can get creative with it. To accomplish this, you'll make three colorful homemade syrups to be served and mixed with seltzers and garnishes. To achieve the theme, dress a small table up with spiderwebs and any other skeletons you can dig out from the closet (not the metaphorical kind!). Use unexpected serveware, such as Halloween cauldrons with ice, punch bowls and ladles, liquid measuring cups, miscellaneous squeeze bottles or bottles with pour spouts, borosilicate test tubes in racks, blood bags, biohazard bags, vases, pitchers—whatever you have, the more eclectic the better!

No matter the syrup, the recipe is the same for each drink: Fill a clear cup with ice. Pour 2 tablespoons of syrup, more or less to taste, and top off with seltzer and your desired garnish.

"Horseshoe Crab Blood" Coconut Milk Syrup

Makes 2 cups

Atlantic horseshoe crabs were once plentiful at Fort Tilden Beach in New York City. For parts of the warm season, I'd observe their spiky bodies that looked like decorative, dystopian alien armor and marvel at what the milky sky-blue color of their blood might look like. This syrup emulates that very color. Butterfly pea flower, often used in Thai and Malaysian cooking, has a similarly distinct bright blue color. And when you alter the pH by adding something like lemon juice, acid's famous color-changing abilities are activated and it turns magenta. Magic before your eyes!

3 tablespoons butterfly pea flower tea leaves

¾ cup canned coconut milk

1 cup sugar

1. In a small pot, combine the tea, coconut milk, 1 cup water, and the sugar. Bring the mixture to a boil, then reduce to a low simmer and cook for 10 minutes.

2. Remove the syrup from the heat and strain through a fine-mesh sieve set over a bowl, using a wooden spoon to press out any additional color from the tea. Discard the sieve's contents and funnel the syrup into a bottle.

"Pond Scum" Pandan Syrup

Makes 2 cups

Pandan leaves come from the screwpine fruit tree, which looks similar to a palm tree and is plentiful in tropical climates. The leaves impart a subtle flavor and fragrance often used in Asian roll cakes and sticky rice cake desserts. You can typically find the leaves at Asian grocers in the freezer aisle, stacked and sealed in packs next to the banana leaves. I like to extract the light vanilla, grassy, rice water flavor to make a bright green syrup for sweets and drinks. It's delicious and cozy when added to a warm cup of fresh soy milk, an elegant flavor layer to sweeten an iced matcha latte, or simply straightforward in a spritz.

5 pieces frozen pandan leaves, rinsed and cut into ½-inch pieces

1½ cups sugar

1. In a blender, combine the pandan leaves, sugar, and 1½ cups water. Blend on high speed until the pandan is a fine pulp and the mixture is bright green, 1 to 2 minutes.

2. Pour the mixture into a small pot. Bring to a boil over high heat, then reduce to a simmer and cook for 10 minutes.

3. Let cool slightly, then pour into a fine-mesh sieve set over a bowl. Discard the pulp and funnel the syrup into a bottle.

"Type A Blood" Berry Syrup

This straightforward strawberry syrup is deepened to a blood-colored hue and balanced with the sour of pomegranate syrup (available at any shop that sells Middle Eastern goods).

1½ cups whole strawberries

2 tablespoons pomegranate syrup

1 cup sugar

1. In a small pot, combine the berries, pomegranate syrup, 1 cup water, and the sugar. Bring the mixture to a boil over high heat, then reduce to a low simmer and cook for 10 minutes. While it simmers, smash the berries with a whisk, potato masher, or fork to make a syrupy pulp.

2. Remove the mixture from the heat and cool slightly. With a fine-mesh sieve set over a bowl, use a wooden spoon to press the fruit and drain the syrup. Funnel the syrup into a bottle. Reserve the pulp in a jar for a textured garnish.

Plasma Cocktail

Makes 1

Imagine if a whiskey sour and a Negroni had a baby. The resulting drink is the beloved sweet-and-bitter of the Negroni balanced with a foamy head from an added egg white and a "sour mix" of lemon juice, turbinado sugar, and blood orange juice in the shaker. This is a chic cocktail for entertaining or just for yourself, but it also pairs well with the forthcoming dinner menu. You can prebatch the base in a bottle in your freezer to scale: Just funnel equal parts Campari, gin or mezcal, and sweet vermouth into a bottle and pop it in the freezer. When your friends come over, add the egg white, lemon juice, and blood orange juice to order in the shaker. This is a great task to do with a friend, which takes the pressure off of you and gives folks a way to pitch in! Use square ice cubes for craft-cocktail quality.

Square ice cubes

½ ounce fresh lemon juice

½ ounce fresh blood orange juice, plus more for garnish

1 ounce gin or mezcal

1 ounce Campari

1 ounce sweet red vermouth

1 egg white

½ teaspoon turbinado sugar

Orange zest strip, for garnish

1. Fill a rocks glass with 4 ice cubes and set aside in the freezer.

2. In a cocktail shaker, combine the lemon juice, blood orange juice, all the booze, the egg white, and sugar. Top with about 6 ice cubes. Seal the shaker and shake vigorously for 1 minute, or until you can hear the ice cubes break down a bit. It'll sound slightly slushy, and the shaker will be frosty cold. Your drink is now aerated and super cold.

3. Remove the chilled rocks glass from the freezer and strain the drink into the glass. Shake to get every drop, including the foam.

4. Take a 1 × 3-inch strip of orange zest and fold it in half lengthwise (zest downward with pith side upward) to spray orange oil onto the top of the drink. Drop the zest pith side up to rest on the ice like "skin." Take your blood orange half and squeeze a couple more droplets of juice or "blood" over the top of your drink for a splattered red garnish.

"Rat Brain" Walnut Cookies

Makes 25 cookies

These cookies are an ode to one of my infamous childhood recipes, Crusty Belly Buttons from Tina Vilicich-Solomon's Gross Goodies. *This book was my creed when I was growing up, and these cookies—shortbread thumbprints with jam in the middle (the crusty belly button!)—were my go-to. In this version, I add walnuts two ways: First by deeply roasting them and folding them into the shortbread. Then, by adding a whole walnut (the brain) on top—the brainier the walnut, the better. The brain is then coated in a slick of red raspberry jam, which melts and oozes in the oven, becoming a bloody, chewy glaze. The "blood" looks more convincing if you choose a seedless jam, but the flavor will be equally tasty regardless. Note that you should make the cookie dough at least 3 hours before baking.*

2 sticks (8 ounces) unsalted butter, at room temperature

½ cup granulated cane sugar

1¾ cups all-purpose flour

1 cup finely chopped roasted walnuts

25 whole walnuts, hand-picked for their braininess

⅓ cup raspberry jelly

1. In a stand mixer, cream the butter and sugar until light and voluminous, 1 to 2 minutes. Intermittently scrape the sides down to mix thoroughly.

2. In a medium bowl, briskly whisk the flour for 15 seconds to remove any lumps. Pour the flour and chopped walnuts into the butter mixture and beat until the dough just comes together as a crumbly pile, another 15 seconds, stopping to scrape the sides if needed. No need to overmix since you'll form the dough with your hands next.

3. Pull out a 20-inch sheet of plastic wrap. Fold it over itself to make a rectangular double layer, then tear it off. Cut two 4-inch lengths of butcher's twine and set aside. Using a spatula, scrape and dump all the dough onto the center of the plastic wrap. Use your hands to push the dough into a tightish rectangular shape, about 3 inches wide by 15 inches long. Take the bottom length of plastic wrap and fold it over the dough. Using your fingertips, press the dough into a log while you roll the plastic wrap up and away from you. Aim to get a tight cylinder about 14 inches long by 2½ inches in diameter, with about 4 inches of plastic wrap to spare on either side. Refine the cylinder by twisting the loose plastic wrap ends like a giant candy. On one side of the cylinder, start twisting the end of the plastic wrap against the side of the cookie log. Keep twisting until it's tightened, and tie off with one piece of trimmed twine. Twist the

(continued)

other side of the log tightly and keep twisting. This will force the log to form a tidy cylinder. Tie off this end. Mold the entire log with your hands into a more even cylinder, then go back to the first end and tighten more if you can. You should end up with a neat and firm log. It's mandatory to chill the shortbread log in the refrigerator for at least 3 hours, although overnight or a few days in advance is good, too.

4. Preheat the oven to 325°F. Line two sheet pans with parchment paper.

5. Unwrap the dough and use a sharp knife to slice the chilled dough into ¼-inch-thick rounds. Arrange the sliced cookies on the lined pans, leaving about 1 inch around each cookie. Add 1 whole walnut, flat side down, in the center of each sliced cookie. Using a small teaspoon, scoop a marble-size amount of jelly onto the top of each walnut and with the back of the spoon, slightly flatten to cover the entire top of the walnut. This will help glaze each walnut completely. It's okay if the glaze is slightly messy; each will melt and ooze in a unique way.

6. Bake the cookies until the edges of the cookies lightly brown and the jelly looks slightly tacky, about 25 minutes.

7. Transfer the cookies to a wire rack to cool.

8. To serve, present the rat brain cookies on a clean and shiny cookie sheet, with cooking tweezers alongside. It'll look like a pile of bloody rat brains sitting on a surgical tray with surgical tweezers as serving tongs. Rest in peace, city rats!

Pumpkin Pastillas de Leche

Makes 30 pieces

Pastillas de leche are traditional Filipino gifting candies that are individually wrapped and often given out to friends and family during the holidays. They are customarily made with delicious local water buffalo milk, but condensed milk is an easy substitute in the diaspora. The original candies are creamy-colored logs rolled in crunchy granulated sugar, and sometimes are flavored with ube (purple yam), giving the candies an eye-popping royal purple hue. For Halloween, let's make them winter squash–flavored with steamed, mashed kabocha or butternut squash.

1 cup mashed steamed kabocha squash or butternut squash

¾ cup plus 2 tablespoons sweetened condensed milk

½ cup instant nonfat dry milk

¼ teaspoon finely grated lime zest

1 teaspoon kosher salt

2 tablespoons sugar, plus more for rolling and shaping

1. In a medium fry pan, combine the mashed squash and condensed milk and cook over medium heat until thickened and jammy, 6 to 8 minutes. Add the dry milk, lime zest, salt, and sugar. Continue cooking and stirring until slightly thickened, about 3 minutes. Transfer to a small bowl and cover with plastic wrap pressed onto the surface of the squash mixture. Let cool.

2. Turn the mixture out onto a work surface and roll into a 1-inch-wide log. The dough will have a texture like Play-Doh, but softer. Sprinkle generous amounts of sugar over the work surface to help with sticking and roll the logs in sugar until liberally coated. Keep adding sugar until you achieve the right consistency. It should be soft but able to maintain its shape.

3. Line a baking sheet with parchment paper. To make pumpkin-shaped candies, cut the log into 1-inch lengths and roll each piece into a ball while coating it in sugar. Using your fingertips, press each piece into various pumpkin shapes. Use any helpful kitchen tools, like table knives or chopsticks, to shape the pumpkin ridges or make jack-o-lantern designs.

4. Transfer each pumpkin candy to the lined baking sheet, which has been sprinkled with some more sugar. Cover with plastic wrap and transfer to the refrigerator. Once chilled, the pastillas are ready to eat. They will keep in the fridge for up to 1 month. Serve on a plate.

Bonus Step: If you're feeling extra festive, serve these on a "pumpkin patch." Plant the pumpkin candies on top of a sheet pan lined with the classic illusion of crushed Oreo cookie soil. Maybe add some wheatgrass sticking out of the soil and arrange some cleaned and scrubbed small rocks of various sizes to the dessert landscape.

Hot Dog Fingers

Makes 16 fingers

In New York City, you either boil or pan-sear your hot dogs. (We lovingly call a boiled hot dog a "water dog.") If you're going the pan-sear route, take a cue from the steam-frying method of cooking dumplings (first you fry lightly in oil, then you add water and cover to steam and cook it all the way through). If you have veggie friends in attendance, bring veggie dogs, or cut some carrots in the shape of fingers and roast them in the oven until they are soft and charred. For buns, I like them soft and fluffy, straight out of the bag.

16 hot dogs (I prefer Nathan's)
3 tablespoons neutral oil
  (if steam-frying)
16 sliced almonds
16 hot dog buns (still in their bags)
Condiments

1. For water dogs, bring a large pot of water to a boil. If you're steam-frying, skip this step.

2. For each hot dog, use a paring knife to make three lines across the middle of the hot dog to resemble a knuckle. Make a slit at one end of each hot dog, wide and deep enough to fit an almond slice to be a fingernail. Set the hot dogs aside.

3. For the steam-fried dogs: Heat a heavy-bottomed fry pan over medium-high heat. Add a splash of oil and layer 4 to 6 hot dogs in the pan to sear. Add a lid to cover the pan and sear for about 2 minutes. Remove the lid and flip each hot dog, quickly adding 2 tablespoons of water to the pan and replacing the lid. Fry for another 2 minutes. The hot dogs should have expanded and curled to reveal the knuckle wrinkles you carved out. Transfer to a plate and repeat with the remaining hot dogs.

4. For water dogs: Plop 8 hot dogs at a time into the boiling water. Lower the heat to medium for a gentle boil. Boil the hot dogs until curled, 3 to 4 minutes. Transfer to a plate and repeat with the remaining hot dogs.

5. Lay the hot dogs knuckle side up to present as fingers—they should be gnarled and imperfect, resembling jammed fingers. Slide a sliced almond into the nail bed of each hot dog and secure it by slightly puncturing the hot dog with the wide end of the almond slice.

6. Serve the hot dogs buffet style, with buns straight out the bag so they don't harden, and an array of condiments, sillily renamed for the occasion.

"Monster Fur" Corn Cakes

Makes 12 corn cakes

These sweet, custardy cake-based cookies are a variation of Filipino corn bibingka (typically made with rice flour) and Mexican pan de elote—both familiar flavors from growing up in the Filipino and Mexican neighborhoods of east side San Jose, California. Topped with dried corn silk fried in brown butter—a happy accident I discovered while recipe testing—they are perfectly monster-esque.

Corn Silk "Monster Fur"

2 cups corn silk, reserved from 5 ears and dried on a sheet pan

4 ounces butter or ghee

kosher salt

Corn Cakes

3 cups corn kernels, shucked from 5 ears (reserve corn silk)

One 14-ounce can condensed milk

½ teaspoon vanilla extract

4 tablespoons butter, at room temperature

3 medium eggs

3 tablespoons fine masa harina

1 teaspoon baking powder

½ teaspoon kosher salt

Softened butter for the pan

Glaze

1 cup powdered sugar

2 to 4 tablespoons milk

1. Preheat the oven to 350°F.

2. Make the corn silk "monster fur": On a plate, fluff the dried corn silk, making sure there aren't any tangled patches.

3. Line a separate plate with paper towels and have near the stove. Heat a deep pan over medium-high heat. Add the butter or ghee and swirl until the it is completely liquefied and shimmers.

4. Quickly add half the corn silk and fluff in the pan to evenly fry. The corn silk should frizzle and smell nutty in a few seconds. Remove the corn hair with a fork, then separate on a paper towel to cool. Sprinkle with a little pinch of salt. Repeat with the other half. Control the heat by taking the pan off and on, being careful not to burn. Set aside.

5. Make the corn cakes: In a blender, combine the corn, condensed milk, vanilla, and butter and puree for 30 seconds. Add the eggs and puree for another 10 seconds. Finally, add the masa harina, baking powder, and salt and pulse for a couple more seconds until just blended.

6. Use a brush to grease 12 cups of a muffin tin with the softened butter. Ladle about ⅓ cup of the corn cake batter into each.

7. Bake until the top of each cake is lightly browned and puffy, about 30 minutes.

8. Let the cakes cool in the tin for about 10 minutes, then use an offset spatula or table knife to transfer and flip them upside down onto a wire rack to cool. The cakes will flatten once fully cooled.

9. Make the glaze: In a medium bowl, combine the powdered sugar and 2 tablespoons of the milk. Mix with a fork and add more milk 1 tablespoon at a time to achieve a syrupy texture.

10. Once the cakes are cooled, use a teaspoon to slather each cake with a thin layer of the glaze. Top each cake with a pinch of corn silk monster fur in an even layer or scraggly as you wish. Serve on a plate, or if you have a clean furry cloth lying around, arrange the cakes in a polka dot pattern to serve.

Run of Show

No matter how simple or involved a gathering is, it never hurts to have an understanding of your programming. How will you navigate transition moments? Who's going to help you bring the party indoors? How does everything evolve . . . or devolve? Given that this gathering doesn't follow the traditional sit-down dinner party format, here's how I recommend you time and space your event.

5:30 p.m.

Inside: The fire kindling is in place, the curry is simmering, and the cocktails are batched and ready.

Outside: Your bestie arrived early and is helping you set up the potion station on a foldable table. You're strategizing where to hang the pabitin (see page 191) while you stream spooky tunes through a portable speaker. (I recommend "Classical Halloween Playlist" on Spotify or an Edgar Allen Poe audiobook reading.) The setup is almost complete.

6:30 p.m.

Outside: Most of your friends have arrived, some with their children and dogs in tow. You explain the goal of pabitin (grab as many treats and prizes as possible) before you start the game. Everyone goes wild.

7:45 p.m.

Outside: The sun is setting and you start to break down your setup. Cart your potion station inside, while setting up an honor system candy bucket at your front door for passersby.

8:00 p.m.

Inside: Light the fire, assign a friend or two to shake the cocktails, start roasting the fennel, and warm up the dishes to get them ready to serve. With the party already in full swing thanks to the Spooky Stoops portion of the evening, the dinner should feel more casual and elastic. Do whatever feels right, whether that's sitting on the floor in the living room with a warm bowl or asking people to serve themselves directly from the pot.

10:00 p.m.

Inside: Do whatever cleanup is necessary for you to get a good night's sleep, but leave as much as possible until morning. What's more important is that you enjoy the lingering presence of your friends and family.

Mimi's Caramelized Fennel, Preserved Lemon & Garlic

Serves 6 to 8

Meriem Bennani, one of my longtime collaborators, is a Moroccan artist based in New York City. Meriem loves food and is an excellent cook. She grew up cooking Moroccan food, so I always learn a lot from her cooking style—especially how she seasons and treats veggies. I once ate something akin to this recipe at a casual dinner she hosted on her rooftop and I was mind-blown, so this is my interpretation of her recipe based simply on sense and memory. The perfect bite includes a piece of roasted garlic, a chunk of fennel, and a piece of caramelized preserved lemon. This dish can be prepped on a sheet pan in advance and roasted right when your guests come in.

1 head garlic, broken up into cloves, peels intact

3 tablespoons olive oil

Salt

4 bulbs fennel, stalks and fronds removed, cored and cut into 1½-inch wedges

4 wedges preserved lemon, cut into ¾-inch bites, with brine

½ fresh lemon, seeded

1. Preheat the oven to 400°F. Line a sheet pan with parchment paper.

2. Set all of the unpeeled garlic cloves on a square of aluminum foil. Drizzle 1 tablespoon of the olive oil on top, season with some salt, and toss gently. Close the foil into a packet, then transfer to the lined pan. Push the garlic packet off to the side of the pan.

3. On the same pan, make a pile of the fennel wedges and preserved lemon chunks. Toss with the remaining 2 tablespoon olive oil and add a couple tablespoons of brine from the preserved lemon jar for good measure. Mix gently with your hands and spread out evenly on the pan.

4. Roast for about 25 minutes. Open the garlic foil packet and sprinkle the whole cloves (with their skins intact) across the pan to join the rest of the roasting veggies. Roast until the fennel and preserved lemon are caramelized and browned, another 10 to 15 minutes. Squeeze on some fresh lemon juice and serve.

Nashi Pear, Jicama & Toasted Hazelnut Salad

Serves 6 to 8

Once, for a big twelve-course artist dinner, I made a huge batch of ginger candies for a welcome cocktail garnish. The preparation was intensive: peeling, slicing, braising in sugar syrup, and drying 120 thin coins of ginger. The powerful ginger candy garnish stood on its own as a foil to a smoky, sour, mezcal/tamarind/lime cocktail. The leftover candies ended up saving the day when I decided to try a first-time experiment with a nashi pear salad. I knew it was missing one note, and at the last minute before the salads went out, I quickly minced the ginger and sprinkled it on top of the salad. It became an instant classic. Because I love you, this recipe does not require that you candy your own ginger, but now you know the origin story.

Layer the ingredients like a tray of nachos so each juicy pear or jicama gets a roasty, crunchy bite of hazelnut and a chewy zing of candied ginger.

1 nashi (Asian) pear, peeled, cored, and cut into ¼-inch slices

½ pound jicama, peeled and cut into ¼-inch slices

¼ cup roasted hazelnuts, coarsely chopped

2 tablespoons finely minced candied ginger

2 tablespoons hazelnut oil

2 tablespoons rice vinegar

Flaky salt

On a large, flat plate or two, arrange alternating shingles of sliced pear and jicama. Sprinkle the chopped hazelnuts and candied ginger evenly over the entire surface of the salad. Finally, drizzle the hazelnut oil and rice vinegar over the top and sprinkle with flaky salt.

Pumpkin & Plantain Curry

Serves 6 to 8

In 2019, I helped open a resort for The Standard Hotels in the Maldives as Creative Director of Food and Culture. Getting there meant a nearly 24-hour flight consisting of two jets and a thin-walled 12-seat airboat, so naturally I was exhausted by the time I arrived. In a happy coincidence, my dusk arrival coincided with the breaking of Ramadan fast. I was greeted with a huge glass of salty-sweet Maldivian watermelon juice and the most memorable plate of yellow curry. It was my first time having curry with local bananas. It was a welcome change from potato—sweet and tender—while still imparting a rich curry flavor.

Over my various works trips to the Maldives, I came to describe the cuisine as similar to Sri Lankan food, but with tropical ingredients and plentiful fish. This recipe is my fall homage to the staff meal of my dreams.

Curry Paste

1 teaspoon cumin seeds, toasted
6 garlic cloves
1 thumb of fresh ginger, sliced
1 medium white onion, chopped
4 curry leaves
1 small Thai chile

Curry Base

2 tablespoons coconut oil
1 medium red onion, cut into ½-inch chunks
2 teaspoons salt, plus more as needed
2 cinnamon sticks
1 teaspoon ground turmeric
4 cardamom pods, smashed
1 teaspoon cumin seeds, toasted
3 makrut lime leaves
2 sweet plantains, cut into 1-inch chunks
3 small delicata squash, seeded and cut into ½-inch half-moons
1 large Thai chile, sliced

For Serving

1 bunch of fresh cilantro, coarsely chopped
Coarsely ground black pepper

To Finish

One 13.5-ounce can coconut milk
½ pound fresh tuna, cut into 1-inch cubes
1 thumb of fresh ginger, julienned
1½ teaspoons fish sauce
1½ teaspoons turbinado sugar

1. Make the curry paste: In a blender, combine 1 cup water, the cumin seeds, garlic, ginger, white onion, curry leaves, and chile. Blend for 1 minute, or until it comes together as a smooth paste. Set aside.

2. Make the curry base: Heat a large, heavy-bottomed pot over medium-high heat. Add the coconut oil, red onion, and salt and cook for 5 minutes to soften slightly. Add the cinnamon sticks, turmeric, cardamom, cumin seeds, and whole makrut lime leaves. Stir to toast for about 1 minute.

3. Add the curry paste and 2 cups water and bring to a boil. Add the sweet plantains, squash, Thai chile, and salt to taste. Bring to a boil, then reduce heat to a low simmer and cook until the vegetables have softened, about 15 minutes.

4. Finish the curry: Add the coconut milk, tuna, and ginger, then season with the fish sauce and turbinado sugar. Simmer for about 5 minutes, until the tuna just cooks. Adjust the sauce consistency with water if needed.

5. Garnish with the fresh cilantro and coarsely ground black pepper.

Soy-Cured Egg Yolks

Makes 6 to 8

Imagine the pleasure of runny egg yolks firmed with a savory hit of soy sauce. That's what these yolks are, and they're amazing as an elegant sauce tipped into steamed rice or boiled noodles. Have a couple extra eggs on hand (in case you break any!) and save the whites (they keep in the fridge in an airtight container for up to 2 weeks) to make the Plasma Cocktail (page 194).

6 to 8 large eggs, refrigerator-cold
6 to 8 teaspoons soy sauce

1. Give an egg a gentle tap on a hard work surface or kitchen counter. Pour the egg into one hand while you steady the yolk on your fingers. Let the remaining white slip through your fingers and into a container to save for later use.

2. Carefully slide the yolk back into one half of the shell without popping it. Add a teaspoon of soy sauce and swirl gently so that the soy sauce runs under the yolk. Stand the shell with the yolk up in the egg carton. Repeat with the rest of the eggs. (You may pop some yolks or end up with unevenly cracked shells in the process. If that happens, save those eggs with the whites and reserve them all for another use.)

3. Close the egg carton top and refrigerate for 2 to 3 hours to allow the yolks to cure.

Hamman Bay Leaf Rice

Serves 6 to 8

There's no other fragrance and feeling quite like when you first open a pot of freshly steamed rice. Even better, you can elevate it to the point where it's just like experiencing an aromatherapy-infused facial. This is achieved by adding an unusual twist: a generous amount of bay leaf powder to your rice. The result is a uniquely fragrant rice dish with eucalyptus-like aromas, complemented by the grassy and citrusy notes of dill, all enhanced by a finish of the gilded, rich dribble of soy-cured egg yolks.

6 dried bay leaves

1½ cups Japanese sushi rice

½ cup red quinoa

6 fresh bay leaves, plus more for garnish

½ cup ghee or unsalted butter, melted

Kosher salt

Dill sprigs

6 to 8 Soy-Cured Egg Yolks (page 208)

1. Use a spice grinder or mortar and pestle to grind the dried bay leaves into a fine powder.

2. In a rice cooker bowl, combine the rice and quinoa and add enough cold water to cover by 1 inch. Massage the rice and quinoa with your hands, then carefully pour out the water, leaving the rice mixture behind. Repeat until the water runs clear, about 2 more times. Add the fresh bay leaves, dried bay leaf powder, and 1¾ cups water. Stir well, then put the bowl in the rice cooker and set to cook.

3. Just before serving, pour the ghee over the rice and quinoa. Use a rice paddle to loosen the rice-quinoa mixture and stir until the ghee is evenly incorporated. Season to taste with salt, then spread on a serving platter and scatter dill on top.

4. Nestle the egg yolks in their shells into the mixture. Garnish with more fresh bay leaves, instructing your guests to not eat them. Serve immediately, giving each guest one yolk with an equal portion of rice and telling them to tip the yolk onto the rice and mix it in before eating.

Pabitin

A treat-grabbing game that literally means "rack of goodies."

    You can easily construct your own pabitin and decorate it to your liking. The beauty is that it is totally scalable, customizable, and reusable! Essentially, a pabitin is a simple grid made of bamboo sticks that is decorated with crepe paper tassels and strung up with candies and prizes. Unlike its cousin the piñata, the pabitin activates our magpie tendencies. It's a visual overload, a grab-it-all feast for your eyes and your hands. The more diversity in decorations the better, which makes this a great opportunity to clean out your junk drawer and put all those random ribbons and tissues you've saved from gifts and packages to good use.

Six 3-foot bamboo sticks
Baker's twine
Crepe paper tassels
Hanging pom-poms
Recycled ribbons
Cellophane baggies
Candies and prizes

1. On a flat surface, lay three bamboo sticks 3 feet equidistant from each other. Lay the remaining bamboo sticks on top and perpendicular to the ones you just laid, creating a 3 × 3-foot grid. Using the baker's twine, secure the bamboo in place with sturdy knots. Any will do, but if you want to look up a reliable knot, search "lashing knot" for this step.

2. Decorate your grid with tassels, pom-poms, ribbons—whatever you have on hand to make it visually stimulating and full! Intersperse the decorations with cellophane baggies full of homemade (or store-bought) candies, treats, and whatever other prizes you want to include.

3. To play, string the pabitin up so that it can be lifted and lowered by the game operators. Keep the structure moving up and down while the kids, adults, or dogs jump to claim their rewards.

Canine Edition: To make this into a dog-friendly version, simply substitute dog bones and tennis balls for the candies and toys. The pups will love it!

4 OR MORE DAYS OUT

Prep the pabitin (see opposite).

Make the cookie dough and keep in the freezer; set aside the walnuts for topping.

Make the pastillas and keep in the fridge; crush the Oreo cookie "soil."

Prepare drink bar syrups.

Mince ginger and ginger candy for the salad.

Set your fire.

3 DAYS OUT

Batch the cocktail; keep in the freezer.

2 DAYS OUT

Bake the cookies.

Measure out the corn cake ingredients.

Score the hot dogs.

Make the curry base sans vegetables; keep in fridge.

1 DAY OUT

Bake the corn cakes.

Prep the sheet pan for roasting the fennel.

Cut the curry vegetables; measure the remaining ingredients to toss in tomorrow.

Prepare the herbs for the rice.

DINNER PARTY!

Consult your handy Run of Show (page 202).

Decorate the stoop and hang the pabitin.

Glaze the corn cakes, fry the corn hair, and garnish the corn cakes.

Cook the hot dogs.

Prep the salad.

Simmer the curry.

Steam and season the rice.

Light the fire before dinner.

A Better Friendsgiving

WITH KIA DAMON

Kia Damon is a Florida-born chef, writer, host, and recipe developer. Her work has taken her from founding The Supper Club from Nowhere to being Cherry Bombe's first Culinary Director to her own cookbook *Cooking with Florida Water*. Her work is a love letter to her roots and an attempt to bring cultures together. The best part? You can taste it.

STEAL
MY
PLAYLIST

November doesn't get the love she deserves, and I'm definitely, totally, for sure not just saying that because I was born on November 22 with two of my big three astrological placements in Sagittarius. I'm speaking factually, objectively, with zero bias—which means you can trust my word. I promise. In the game of dinner parties, the summer and spring months almost always clean house.

The weather does the majority of the work, and folks already have the serotonin levels necessary to leave the house armed with a bottle of orange wine in one hand, crusty loaf of bread in the other. Sandwiched between the early crisp, pumpkin-filled energy of October and the end of the year, bundle-weather buzz of December, November often feels like it stands alone as a buffer month. Through no fault of its own, November is home to the loaded holiday known as Thanksgiving and its slightly less problematic cousin, Friendsgiving.

Ah yes, Friendsgiving. A holiday where your friends come by with their renditions of holiday classics such as greens, banana pudding, mac 'n' cheese, et cetera. You know it's not going to be as good as your grandmother's cooking, but we pretend that it's just as good, because we're trying to do good by calling it Friendsgiving instead of Thanksgiving.

If my memory serves me correctly, Friendsgiving was my first introduction to dinner parties. I didn't really grow up in a dinner party household. We ate for holidays, special after-church occasions at the local buffet, and Super Bowl parties that usually involved hot wings and my dad grilling burgers past well done. When I moved from home to Tallahassee, my newfound friends were broke college students living within a mile of the campus. It was when I met them that I became accustomed to the concept of showing up to someone else's home for hot food, cheap wine, and hard ciders. Back then, we simply called it "getting together." November would mosey along and the group chat was moving a million texts a minute sorting who would be in town, who's making vegan mac 'n' cheese, and who's hosting a group of twenty-year-olds in their college apartment. It was truly the highlight of my early twenties and I look back fondly on it all. The store-bought chicken from Publix, the sweet Hawaiian dinner rolls, PBR by the pack. Playing records with random music videos on silently in the background, perfect for when the edible kicked in, gluing you to the couch. Ah, to be young, newly radicalized, and on a budget.

I'm older now, on the horizon of my thirties, and have slightly more budget to work with. Yet, Friendsgivings don't hit like they used to. I want more for us. I cannot sit idly by for another thrown-together potluck. If we are beholden to Friendsgiving, I at least want to put some oomph behind it. *The Princess Diaries* makeover scene pressed into an oil-based essence and dabbed on your wrists and collar bone. Give it a certain je ne sais quoi—an "it" girl energy. A look that says "I actually just threw this all together on a whim even though I look like I'm fresh off the runway." Hence, A Better Friendsgiving. We'll take the base that already exists and simply enhance it. A concealer here, a liquid blush there, a well-curated playlist, and some perfectly cooked beef tenderloin will get us exactly where we need to be.

The recipes in this chapter are a step to the left of your typical holiday fare. You won't find any turkey or casseroles, nor will you be asked to grab a can of gelatinous cranberry sauce. A Better Friendsgiving isn't asking you to call your aunt for that oyster stuffing recipe that you know you aren't going to nail. You also don't need to buy the most expensive serving plates—the food will shine no matter the dinnerware. All you'll truly need is some solid planning, a great friend group, and the optimism of a Sagittarius.

Cranberry Spritz

Makes 16 cocktails

Two things can be true: Canned cranberry sauce can be unappealing and fresh cranberries can be a delight. It didn't feel right to completely erase cranberry from the Friendsgiving agenda, so I found a better home for her among the beverage options. I'm a nonalcoholic girly, hence the club soda and sparkling grape juice. If you're feeling boozy, opt for prosecco or Champagne. Enjoy all fall and winter.

2 oranges
2 cups fresh cranberries
2 cups sugar
1 cinnamon stick
2 whole star anise
2 sprigs fresh thyme
Ice
1 liter club soda
1 bottle sparkling white grape juice

Make Ahead: You can make the syrup up to 1 month in advance and store in an airtight container in the refrigerator.

1. With a vegetable peeler, pull off a strip of orange zest 2 inches long. Cut the rest of the orange into slices to use as a garnish and set aside.

2. In a large pot, combine the orange zest, cranberries, sugar, cinnamon stick, star anise, thyme, and 4 cups water and bring to a boil. Reduce to a simmer and cook until the cranberries burst and the liquid reduces by half, about 8 minutes. Strain the syrup, discarding the solids, and let it cool completely.

3. To assemble a drink, fill a short glass or coupe with ice, drizzle in 2 tablespoons of the syrup, and top with club soda or sparkling grape juice. Finish the rim with an orange slice rubbed along it for fun.

Buttermilk & Rosemary Roast Chicken

Serves 6 to 8

Skip the traditional turkey in favor of this spatchcocked roast chicken. It does everything you want the turkey to do but with less work and more flavor. The magic of this recipe lies in the power of buttermilk. It acts as a double agent, imparting flavor but also deeply tenderizing the chicken, a dish that's known for being disappointingly dry. Breathe new life into this bird and watch it fly from the platter.

1 whole chicken (3 to 4 pounds)

Kosher salt

1 quart full-fat buttermilk

1 tablespoon Tabasco sauce

3 sprigs fresh rosemary, picked and finely chopped

2 large yellow onion, halved and cut into ¼-inch slices

10 garlic cloves, smashed

1. To ensure the chicken is cooked evenly, we're going to spatchcock it, creating more surface area for the heat to touch. First, flip the bird onto its breast. Holding it steady from the top, use kitchen shears to cut to the right of the tailpiece and follow the backbone right up to the neck opening. Repeat on the other side and then pull out the backbone. Once it's removed, flip the chicken breast side up and press your hands down on the splayed chicken breast like you're performing CPR.

2. Salt the chicken all over and in the cavity. In a small bowl, stir together the buttermilk, Tabasco, and rosemary. Pour the mixture over the chicken in a zip-seal bag large enough to hold it comfortably. Put the bag in a bowl and place it in the refrigerator. Let it brine overnight, flipping the bag halfway through to ensure every part gets a chance to be submerged.

3. When you're ready to cook, preheat the oven to 400°F.

4. Spread the onion and garlic evenly on the bottom of a large roasting pan. Remove the chicken from the brine and scrape a considerable amount of the excess off. Lay the chicken on top and slide it into the oven on the middle rack.

5. Roast until the internal temperature reaches 165°F, 50 minutes to 1 hour, rotating the pan front to back halfway through. To keep the chicken from browning too much before it's finished cooking, you can cover it with a tent of aluminum foil.

6. Be sure to let the chicken rest for at least 15 minutes before serving.

Roasted Beef Tenderloin with Beurre Blanc

Serves 10 to 12

In the movie Ratatouille, *the good conscience apparition of Auguste Gusteau has a saying he repeats throughout the film: "What I say is true—anyone can cook, but only the fearless can be great." I'm going to ask that you be fearless when you cook this dish. I need you to rely on instinct, your attention to detail, and have a bit of bravado. A meat thermometer will be your best friend here since temperature plays a major part in achieving that ratio of crusty outside to tender inside. Mise your ingredients for the beurre blanc so you can flow from start to finish, and remember to connect to the little chef that lives within you.*

3- to 4-pound beef tenderloin, trimmed and tied with butcher twine

Kosher salt and freshly cracked black pepper

3 tablespoons olive oil

¼ cup diced shallot

⅓ cup white wine vinegar

⅓ cup dry white wine

½ cup heavy cream

2 sticks (8 ounces) unsalted butter, cut into cubes and chilled

Thinly sliced fresh chives or chopped flat-leaf parsley

Flaky salt

1. Sprinkle the tenderloin with kosher salt and black pepper on all surfaces and chill, covered, in the refrigerator overnight. This helps build a great crust on the outside. Remove the loin from the fridge at least 3 hours before you're ready to cook and let it come to room temperature.

2. Preheat the oven to 425°F.

3. In an extra-large cast-iron pan, heat the olive oil over medium-high heat. If you don't have a large cast-iron, you can cut the meat into two pieces. Sear each side of the meat until a brown crust forms, about 3 minutes per side.

4. Transfer the pan to the oven and roast for 20 to 22 minutes. Use a meat thermometer to check for your ideal temperature. For medium-rare perfection, look for an internal temperature of 120° to 125°F. Let the meat rest for 15 minutes.

5. Meanwhile, in a saucepan or medium pot, combine the shallot, vinegar, and wine and bring to a boil. Reduce to a steady simmer and cook until there's about 3 tablespoons of liquid left, about 5 minutes. Strain the shallot and discard. Return the liquid to the pot.

6. Off the heat, slowly stream in the heavy cream while whisking, making sure to fully incorporate. Return the pot to a very low heat and whisk in the butter 2 cubes at a time. Take your time with this step! You want each cube to have time to melt and emulsify with the heavy cream. The resulting beurre blanc should be a creamy, tangy, silky sauce.

7. Slice the tenderloin into ¼-inch-thick rounds and arrange on a platter. Dress with the beurre blanc and any meat juices in the pan. Garnish with the herbs. Top with flaky salt and more cracked pepper, if desired.

Black-Eyed Pea Salad

Serves 6

All of my life, I've only eaten black-eyed peas one way: piping hot, super savory, flavored with the best smoked meat five bucks can buy. It wasn't until rather recently that I wanted to see black-eyed peas in a new, more refreshing light. An entire salad of starchy peas can seem daunting, but the trio of crunchy and acidic vegetables keeps the palate fatigue at bay. If you can, I encourage you to make this a day ahead so the flavors can mingle and get cozy. I have enough sense to know I didn't invent the black-eyed pea salad, but I can declare with confidence that my rendition is just as delicious as the one you fell in love with. These ain't your grandma's black-eyed peas.

1 pound dried black eyed peas
3 stalks celery, cut into ¼-inch dice
3 scallions, cut into ½-inch rounds
½ small red onion, finely diced
½ cup extra-virgin olive oil
½ cup white wine vinegar or champagne vinegar
Kosher salt

1. Place the peas in an extra-large bowl with enough warm water to cover them by 4 inches. Soak them for 45 minutes. This step can be done the day before if you need to get ahead; they can soak overnight in the fridge.

2. While the beans soak, prep all the vegetables and set aside in a bowl.

3. Drain the peas. In a large pot, combine the peas with fresh water to cover by a couple of inches and bring to a boil. Reduce to a simmer and cook until the beans are al dente (not mushy!), 30 to 35 minutes.

4. Drain the peas and dump them onto a baking tray or dish. Let them cool for at least 1 hour, until fully cooled. You can do this in the fridge or on the counter, dealer's choice.

5. To the bowl of cut-up vegetables, add the cooled peas, olive oil, and vinegar and carefully combine with a spatula. The most efficient method is to pull from the bottom and then fold over the top until everything is homogenous. The key is to avoid breaking or mushing the peas.

6. Season with salt to taste and enjoy the versatility of black-eyed peas.

Sweet Potatoes & Caviar

Serves 4 to 6

This recipe is the culinary embodiment of putting on earrings and lip gloss with your sweatpants: You're just barely put together, but you turn heads nonetheless. My favorite thing about this recipe is that it's hands-off until you need to serve. Roast the potatoes ahead of time and let them rest in their sweetness while your guests get cozy. And don't let the caviar addition spook you! Ask your fishmonger for lumpfish caviar, a cheaper alternative to classic ossetra. Low effort, high impact, baby!

4 to 5 large
  sweet potatoes
Olive oil
Kosher salt
8 ounces crème fraîche
3½ ounces caviar
Minced fresh chives

1. Position racks in the top third and center of the oven and preheat the oven to 425°F.

2. Scrub the sweet potatoes and pat them dry. Using a fork, carefully but forcefully puncture holes in the skin. Drizzle each potato with some olive oil and sprinkle with a few pinches of salt. Wrap each potato individually in foil and twist the ends securely. Place the potatoes on the top rack and set a sheet pan on the rack underneath to catch any drippings.

3. Roast until tender, about 1 hour. Let the potatoes rest 10 minutes before unwrapping.

4. Slice the potatoes open and fluff with a fork. Top each with some crème fraîche, a scoop of caviar, and a sprinkling of chives.

Garlicky Herb Corn Bread

Serves 8

Corn bread is the simplest of the holiday dish lineup, which, unfortunately, leads to it being the most challenging to nail. Nothing hurts like seeing a pan of untouched corn bread, and I want to help you avoid that heartbreak. I learned that the key to corn bread is maintaining moisture from start to finish. That's why I've been adding canned creamed corn to my batter for years now. Once you master the moisture, sky's the limit for flavor combinations. This version has garlic galore, but if you want a seafood restaurant chain vibe, grate cheddar into the batter. If you're yearning for a kick, try 2 tablespoons of diced jalapeño.

1½ cups all-purpose flour

1½ cups plus 3 tablespoons stone-ground yellow cornmeal

3 tablespoons fresh thyme leaves, finely chopped

2 teaspoons baking powder

½ teaspoon baking soda

1 tablespoon sugar

½ teaspoon kosher salt

2 large eggs

1¼ cups whole milk

One 14-ounce can creamed corn

3 garlic cloves, finely minced

2 sticks (8 ounces) plus 2 tablespoons unsalted butter, melted

Butter, for serving

1. Preheat the oven to 400°F.

2. In a large bowl, whisk together the flour, 1½ cups of the cornmeal, the thyme, baking powder, baking soda, sugar, and salt.

3. In a medium bowl, lightly beat the eggs. Add the milk, creamed corn, and garlic and whisk together well.

4. Use a rubber spatula to fold the wet ingredients into the dry ingredients until there aren't any dry pockets. The batter will thicken up.

5. Measure out 3 tablespoons of the melted butter and set aside. Stir the remaining melted butter into the batter until well combined.

6. Over medium heat, pour the reserved melted butter into a nonstick pan, and when it begins to bubble, sprinkle the remaining 3 tablespoons cornmeal evenly across the pan. Pour the batter into the pan and use a spoon or spatula to even it out on the top. Let the batter cook on the stovetop for 2 minutes before transferring to the oven.

7. Bake until a golden crust forms, 25 to 30 minutes. Let rest for 10 minutes before cutting. Serve with more butter, of course.

Punched-Up Green Beans

Serves 4 to 6

Green bean casserole: OUT. Snappy green beans in vinegar with crunchy shallots: IN. It's not that I don't like green bean casserole, it's just that I don't like green bean casserole. There are better ways of preparation that take a fraction of the time. All you need is 6 minutes to trim the beans, make four knife passes over the garlic, and slice the onion for garnish. Set aside another 7 minutes to cook and you have a cute side dish in under 15 minutes.

2 tablespoons olive oil

1½ to 2 pounds green beans, trimmed

3 garlic cloves, diced

2 teaspoons red pepper flakes

1 tablespoon Chinese black vinegar

1 small white onion

1 cup store-bought fried shallots

Kosher salt

1. In a large pan, heat the olive oil over medium heat until shimmering. Add the green beans and cook, stirring often, until the flesh begins to shine and blister, about 5 minutes.

2. Toss in the garlic and reduce the heat to avoid burning it. Continue to cook for another 2 minutes. Add the pepper flakes and vinegar and stir to evenly coat.

3. Cut the white onion in half, then again into quarters. Shave one quarter into ultra-thin slices—ideally on a mandoline. Sprinkle evenly over the top and follow with the fried shallots.

4. Taste for salt and serve immediately or at room temperature.

Citrus & Custard Pavlova

Serves 10

Of all the recipes in this chapter, this is the most difficult. I apologize in advance. As a hostess with the mostest, I cannot resist providing my guests with ye olde razzle-dazzle. Pavlovas are a bit of an event, but that's just because they're so sensitive (which isn't a bad thing!). There's a cheat within reach if you don't feel like making your own curd. Just buy some from the grocery store and pop it out when you're ready to assemble.

4 large eggs, separated

1 cup plus 1 tablespoon superfine sugar

2 teaspoons vanilla extract

1 teaspoon cornstarch

½ teaspoon cream of tartar

¾ cup grapefruit juice

1 cup granulated sugar

6 tablespoons unsalted butter, sliced and chilled

1 cup heavy cream, well chilled

½ pound sweet oranges, peeled and cut into pieces, preferably supremed

Fresh mint leaves, for garnish

Flaky salt (optional)

Make Ahead: Follow steps 1 through 5 to make the pavlova. Store in an airtight container up to 48 hours in advance. Do not store it in the refrigerator, as it will go soft. Make the grapefruit curd up to 2 days in advance and store in an airtight container in the refrigerator.

1. Preheat the oven to 350°F. Line a baking sheet with parchment.

2. In a stand mixer fitted with the whisk, beat the egg whites on medium-high speed until they have soft peaks, 5 to 7 minutes. Carefully add ½ cup of the superfine sugar and beat for 1 minute. Add ½ cup of the remaining superfine sugar and beat for another minute. Turn the mixer to high and beat until the mixture becomes shiny and the peaks are really stiff. Add the vanilla toward the end.

3. With a rubber spatula, carefully fold in the cornstarch and cream of tartar. Try not to mix any of the air out.

4. Use the same spatula to scrape the mixture onto the lined baking sheet. Ideally, you want it in the shape of an 8-inch-ish round with a decent amount of height. Add some swoops for dramatic effect and to hold the toppings.

5. Transfer the pavlova to the oven and reduce the oven temperature to 200°F. Bake for 1 hour 30 minutes, then turn the oven off. Leave the pavlova in the oven without opening the door. Let it cool for at least 3 hours or overnight.

6. Meanwhile, in a saucepan, combine the grapefruit juice and granulated sugar. Stir over medium heat and mix well. In a bowl, beat the egg yolks, then slowly stream them into the grapefruit mixture and whisk steadily for about 5 minutes. (The key is to not turn them into scrambled eggs.) It should begin to thicken. Remove from the heat and whisk in the butter 1 tablespoon at a time, taking care to fully combine after each.

7. Strain through a fine-mesh sieve into a bowl, discard the bits, and set aside to cool.

8. When you're ready to serve the pavlova, in a bowl, with an electric mixer, whisk the heavy cream and remaining 1 tablespoon superfine sugar until it becomes thick and fluffy. Top the pavlova with the curd, followed by the whipped cream and orange segments. Finish with mint leaves for garnish, and add some flaky salt if desired.

Dinner parties are notoriously a lot of work, but when you attend one as a guest, you're often wondering how the host pulled off such a feat. The answer is prep. Ideally you should be preparing for your dinner party at least four days in advance. Everyone's lives are different—your day to day could be vastly different from mine as a chef. What we share, however, is our desire for community and an all-around good time. So, why not make things easier on ourselves?

Here's how I'd break this prep down. Feel free to follow to the T or simply be inspired to create your own.

3 DAYS OUT

Grocery shopping

Prepare cranberry spritz syrup and grapefruit curd.

2 DAYS OUT

Brine chicken.

Make corn bread batter.

Cook black-eyed peas.

Roast sweet potatoes.

1 DAY OUT

Bake corn bread.

Bake pavlova.

Make black-eyed pea salad.

 ### DINNER PARTY!

Roast chicken.

Cook tenderloin.

Cook green beans.

Reheat and finish everything else!

Kia's Clever Substitutes

A key to hosting successfully and authentically is to release yourself from the idea of perfection. Sooner rather than later! Perfection happens when you're able to think quickly and change direction at a moment's notice. Sometimes you realize the lemon in your basket is moldy or your butcher doesn't have the cut of meat you need. Here's a list of replacements and dupes for your dinner party emergencies

No lemon to finish your chicken? Use a tablespoon of sherry vinegar or champagne vinegar. Don't have that? Reach for apple cider or malt vinegar.

In the case that your butcher doesn't have tenderloin, ask for a 3-pound hanger steak and have them clean it for you.

Make a syrup with cranberry juice if all the fresh cranberries have been bought up.

If you aren't too hot on black-eyed peas, canned chickpeas are an excellent swap out. Just give them a good rinse.

Crème fraîche is great but so is old-fashioned sour cream.

No one is going to judge you for swapping the black vinegar for soy sauce or tamari with a splash of apple cider vinegar.

Mama's Da Bin Lo

WITH KEEGAN FONG & MAMA FONG

The mother-son duo behind the beloved Los Angeles restaurant Woon specializes in Chinese comfort food and sharing that food with the world. What started as a pop-up project to showcase Mama Fong's family recipes has now expanded to a vehicle for sharing the Woon story outside the four walls of the restaurant.

Da bin lo! A Chinese phrase meaning "hot pot," which is as fun to eat as it is to say "dah-been-lo." It's a Cantonese saying mainly used by those who hail from Hong Kong, which is where Mama Fong spent her childhood by way of Shanghai. We'd hear my mom say it a few times a year, mainly in the colder months, and almost always to signal a special occasion or that family and friends were coming over. While I believe the excitement over hot pot could be considered a universal phenomenon, the ways we hot pot vary greatly from family to family.

Little nuances and rules of etiquette are what make each family's hot pot their own tradition, and I consider myself honored to share with you Mama Fong's version of da bin lo—the version I grew up with and have now adopted as my own.

Hot pot is a nontraditional way of dining: It requires a group of people huddled around a table engaging and interacting with their food, cooking their ingredients in a boiling pot of broth in the middle of the table. Every guest has to participate because if they don't, then they don't get to eat. However, hard work comes with its rewards, which in this context means not only good food, but a guaranteed good time. Since hot pot is such a communal experience, there's never a dull moment. There's plenty of conversation to be had, music, lots of drinks, and laughter. Hot pot is by nature a dinner party (emphasis on "party"), and like all good dinner parties, it's about the experience and the people around the table. With hot pot you get out of it what you put in (literally and figuratively).

Hot pot is a novel dining experience because of its inherent quality of being, well, hot. That's why we tend to do hot pot in the colder months. It makes you sweat. It steams up your windows—which is also my sign of a successful evening. It has become my family's tradition to da bin lo every Christmas Eve. When we were growing up, most of our friends had prime rib or turkey, but we became known for having Mama Fong's da bin lo. As my sister and I got older, this tradition grew outside of our family. We'd invite a few friends who didn't have family in town to spend the holidays with us. Soon, a few extras at Christmas Eve turned into regular requests for hot pot nights with everyone circled around my mom's round dining table, lazy Susan in the center. Not only is this how our hot pot tradition was born, but it's also how our mom earned her nickname Mama Fong. She'd treat all our friends like her own kids, making sure they were taken care of and had enough to eat. The hot pot nights quickly became a drinking activity that included sake bomb contests (Mama Fong included), where the loser had to eat a chicken foot (sorry, Danny!).

Mama Fong's hot pot is simpler than the familiar Sichuan-style. She provides a straightforward chicken broth that lets the dipping ingredients shine and makes room for her unique sauce offering, which allows each guest to really customize each bite. Although hot pot can seem intimidating, it's not nearly as involved as it looks. We'll outline everything you need to know to make hot pot night a success. Just think of it this way: Everyone technically has to cook their own food, so that takes the pressure off!

As promised, the formula for a good time at hot pot is simple. Make sure to invite good company. Bring lots of drinks—dry Asian beers are preferred (think: Taiwan Beer, Tsingtao, Hite), or hot sake, which famously helps you acclimate to hot environments . . . and also gets you buzzed quicker. Fun tunes are a must; I always prefer to play records, so it gives me the opportunity to get up and stretch when I need to flip sides. (It's a secret tactic: The stretching and moving around allows me to fit more food in my belly.) Most of the time guests are too full to have dessert, but if you can, we always like to polish the evening off with more hot foods like tong yuan, which is black sesame mochi-like balls cooked and served in a warm broth. Like the hot sake, this helps keep your temperature regulated. And if you're anything like my family, make sure to save the leftover broth and ingredients so you can do it all again the next day.

Smashed Radish Salad

Serves 2 or 3

This is a simple and straightforward starter to help cleanse your palate.

1 pound radishes
1 teaspoon kosher salt

Marinade

2 tablespoons Chinese black vinegar
2 tablespoons rice vinegar
2 tablespoons soy sauce
2 tablespoons sugar
1 teaspoon toasted sesame oil
¼ cup chopped scallions

Note: You can prepare this up to 1 to 2 days ahead of time and keep it in the fridge. The longer the radishes sit in the marinade, the better they get!

1. Trim and discard the radish tops and cut the radishes into quarters. Carefully smash each quarter with the back of a fry pan or flat part of a meat tenderizer. Smash the radishes enough to crack them so the marinade is able to soak in, but not too much that they fall apart.

2. Transfer the smashed radishes to a bowl and mix with the salt. Let sit for 15 minutes. Rinse the radishes with water and drain.

3. Make the marinade: In a bowl, stir together both vinegars, the soy sauce, sugar, sesame oil, and scallions.

4. Add the radishes to the marinade and allow the flavors to meld for at least 1 hour before serving.

Mama Fong's Sauce Buffet

Serves 6

The beauty of Mama Fong's da bin lo is that you get to customize your sauce at the sauce station. Some like it spicy while others like it with more vinegar. The sauce is the key to your entire eating experience, so getting it to your preference is important. That said, don't stress too much because you will definitely be getting up multiple times throughout the night to make more sauce at the sauce station. The more times you do it, the more you'll start to develop your preference. The list of sauces below is to prepare a substantial amount of ingredients for your guests to choose from. I've also included my preferred ratio and recipe for sauce (see Sauce Keegan's Way, page 237)—I love extra vinegar and spice.

Arrange the sauce ingredients in an area that is accessible to all guests throughout the evening. Aside from their initial sauce haul, guests will be getting up at different times throughout the dinner to refill their bowl with sauce. Make sure each ingredient has its own spoon for guests to add to their own bowl.

1 cup shacha sauce (preferably Bull Head brand)
1 cup Chinese toasted sesame paste
1 cup garlic chili sauce or Woon Mama's Way Hot Sauce
1 cup regular or Chinese light soy sauce
1 cup distilled white vinegar
½ cup toasted sesame oil
1 cup finely chopped fresh cilantro
1 cup thinly sliced scallions

Choose which of the components you want in your preferred sauce, add to your bowl, and give it all a good mix with your chopsticks at the table. This is the bowl that all your cooked ingredients will land in, mixed in with the sauce. Once the sauce is used up or diluted, it's time to make another trip to the sauce buffet.

SHACHA SAUCE

ADDS: salty, umami, texture, slight spice

BALANCES: sesame oil and sesame paste

CHINESE TOASTED SESAME PASTE

ADDS: creaminess, nuttiness, density

BALANCES: heat from spice, intensity of shacha, acid from vinegar

GARLIC CHILI SAUCE

ADDS: spicy heat, acidity

BALANCES: mellow flavors, savoriness, sesame paste

SOY SAUCE

ADDS: High salinity, umami

Balances: sesame paste, acidity

WHITE VINEGAR

ADDS: acidity, brightness

BALANCES: savoriness, sesame paste

TOASTED SESAME OIL

ADDS: fatty nuttiness, depth of flavor

BALANCES: thickness of the shacha sauce

CILANTRO

ADDS: herby earthiness

SCALLIONS

ADDS: crunch, aromatic sweetness

Sauce Keegan's Way

Serves 1

If you, like me, are of the "more is more" school of thought, then you might want to try my personal sauce recipe to ensure that all your ingredients are covered in sauce. It has a nice balance of everything and more of my favorites (the extra heat of shacha and chili sauces, plus the tanginess of white vinegar). Go ahead and try it! You can always dial it back if you need to.

2 teaspoons shacha sauce

2 teaspoons toasted sesame paste

2 teaspoons garlic chili sauce or Woon Mama's Way Hot Sauce

2 teaspoons distilled white vinegar

1 teaspoon soy sauce (not low-sodium)

1 teaspoon finely chopped fresh cilantro

1 teaspoon thinly sliced scallions

1 teaspoon toasted sesame oil

Add all the ingredients of your choosing to your individual sauce dish and mix.

Mama Fong's Hot Pot

Serves 6

While the sauce is what makes the hot pot experience unique to you, the ingredients are the star of the show. The beauty of hot pot is that all of the raw ingredients can be prepared ahead of time. I'll usually prepare all the ingredients, plate them, wrap them in plastic wrap, and keep them in the fridge until it's time to set the table.

The raw ingredients you offer really depend on how big you want to go. I find that curating the offerings helps the evening run a bit more smoothly. It creates more space on the table and less confusion for any novice hot potters. It also depends on your mood; some days you might want to go heavy on meat, while other days you may want to go heavy on the veggies.

Below is a list of what Mama Fong likes to offer in her da bin lo. It's up to you what you choose from it. I like having variety, but as a general rule of thumb, have about ¼ pound protein per person along with plenty of veggies. I also added a list of some optional ingredients. A word of advice: Plate the ingredients in smaller dishes or bowls so they can all fit on the table and be passed around. Or, if you don't have the space, have a side table for all the ingredients and assign the person closest to the table to pass them around as needed. If hot pot night isn't the perfect excuse to source from your local Asian market, then I don't know what is.

Equipment

1 or 2 tabletop butane burners

1 or 2 butane canisters, plus 1 for backup

1 or 2 large pots

6 "fish nets" or wire mesh baskets

6 medium bowls

Hot Pot

3 pounds napa cabbage

¾ to 1 pound chrysanthemum leaves, rinsed

½ pound dandelion leaves, rinsed

½ pound lotus root, rinsed

5 ounces enoki mushrooms, rinsed and trimmed at the roots

3 pounds precooked Woon Chewy Noodles or your favorite long noodles

¾ to 1 pound salmon fillet

5 ounces fried or regular fish balls, halved

5 ounces Vietnamese meatballs, halved

½ pound firm tofu, cut into ½-inch cubes

1 pound store-bought rib eye rolls

2 quarts chicken or vegetable broth

Dipping Extras

1 pound pork belly, thinly sliced

1 pound chicken, thinly sliced

One 16-ounce package egg dumplings

4 ounces fish cake roll, sliced

4 ounces cellophane or bean thread noodles

1 pound whole shrimp

Note: This recipe serves 6, assuming you are all sharing one pot. If you plan to have additional guests, we recommend using two pots and two burners.

(continued)

1. Cut the head of the napa cabbage lengthwise into quarters and roughly chop each quarter into 1-inch side pieces. Discard the ends. If it's a larger head of cabbage, you can cut into eighths and chop. Rinse, drain, and plate in a large bowl or two smaller bowls.

2. Cut the leaves and thinner stems of the chrysanthemum. Discard the ends and thicker stems. Rinse the leaves, drain, and plate in a larger bowl or two medium bowls.

3. Trim the dandelion leaves, rinse, drain, and plate in a medium bowl.

4. Cut the ends of the rinsed lotus root. Peel the skin and thinly slice into ⅛-inch rounds. Plate in a circle to form a spiral on a small round plate.

5. Rinse and trim the roots of the enoki mushrooms. Plate in a small bowl.

6. To a large pot of boiling water, add the noodles and cook, stirring to keep the noodles separate, for 1½ minutes. Drain and rinse the noodles under cold water to stop the cooking. Drain and plate in a large bowl or two medium bowls.

7. Slice the salmon into pieces 1 to 1½ inches wide and ¼ inch thick. Plate in a circle to form a spiral.

8. Plate the fish balls, meatballs, and tofu in small bowls. Add the rib eye rolls to a small platter, in a stacked pyramid, depending on the serving dish.

9. Pour a 3:1 ratio of broth and water into your Perfect Pot and set over medium-high heat on the stove. Add about one-quarter of the napa cabbage to the broth and bring to a boil. Once it's boiling, transfer the pot to the butane burner.

10. Set a butane burner to high to keep the pot at a boil. Once you start adding ingredients, the temperature of the broth will drop. Keep an eye on the broth throughout the night and turn down or up as needed. The broth level in the pot will decrease slowly throughout the night, so monitor the broth level by adding more boiling water when necessary.

11. Instruct your guests to start adding their desired ingredients into their baskets. Cook times will vary. The general rule of thumb is to add the noodles first and allow them to heat up for about 1 minute. Vegetables, tofu, and salmon cook quickly, about 30 seconds. Meat and lotus root generally take about 1 minute. Use your judgment to feel if something is cooked. More times than not, it will be ready to eat!

Keegan and Mama Fong's Hot Pot Etiquette

Since hot pot is a collective dining experience, there are some dos and don'ts everyone at the table needs to know. Everyone gets their own fish net, aka little wire basket, used to dunk your ingredients into the hot pot and scoop them out. If—god forbid—some ingredients float out of your net and into the communal pot, they are fair game for others. However, pilfering ingredients directly from someone else's fish net is considered the poorest of forms. Second, only get saucy in your own space. Saucing is a highly personalized experience that does not belong in the general pot.

Hot Pot Checklist

Da bin lo is the sum of many, many small parts and moving pieces. Between all the sauces, the plentiful dipping ingredients, and the tableware you'll need to plate them, it can be easy to lose track of a thing or two. That's why we created this handy checklist!

WHAT'S IN A HOT POT KIT?
- 1 or 2 tabletop butane burners
- 1 or 2 butane canisters, plus 1 for backup
- 1 or 2 Perfect Pots
- 6 medium bowls
- 6 sets chopsticks
- 6 "fish nets" or wire mesh baskets
- 6 linen or cloth napkins
- Broth
- Napa cabbage
- Chrysanthemum leaves
- Dandelion leaves
- Lotus root
- Enoki mushrooms
- Woon Chewy Noodles
- Sliced rib eye
- Meatballs
- Fish balls
- Sliced salmon
- Cubed tofu
- All the sauces (see page 236)

Gon Bui!

Gon bui translates to "dry cup" in Cantonese. In other words, drink up! Here are some drink suggestions to keep you cool (or to keep you sweating!) throughout the night.

The Chinese believe it's bad to ingest extremes in your body, like to drink something ice cold while eating something hot. It's supposedly bad for your digestion. But sometimes . . . it's so hot you just need that ice-cold drink to cool you down. (Sorry, mom!)

NIGORI "CLOUDY" SAKE

Nigori sake is best served cold. It's a little sweet and really smooth so it's easy to digest. Sometimes I'll catch myself finishing a bottle way too soon because it goes down way too easily. I prefer the standard Sho Chiku Bai brand because it's pretty affordable and straightforward in taste.

ICE-COLD DRY ASIAN BEER

There is no doubt that an ice-cold beer is the best complement to a hot pot dinner. It's cold and refreshing, which helps balance the heat from the pot. The only downside is that it might fill you up too quickly if you drink too many.

Taiwan Beer	Sapporo	Origin
Classic	Kirin	Hite
Tsingtao	Asahi	Tiger

Warm Drinks

It might sound counterintuitive to drink something warm while you're eating from a hot pot, but the Chinese believe that this is good for your digestion. The other benefit is that it helps you sweat more, which in turn helps you cool down. Not to mention, a warm alcoholic drink while eating warm foods will definitely get you buzzed quicker.

HOT TEA

Hot tea is the best bet for those who prefer to not drink alcohol but still want to help their digestion and break a sweat during the meal. A subtle and smooth oolong or jasmine tea is probably the best complement to a hot pot meal. And trust me, you'll need the caffeine after the amount that you'll be eating.

HOT SAKE

This is definitely my drink of choice for hot pot. For hot sake, *junmai* or "clear" sake is usually preferred. I just heat it up in the microwave for 2 to 3 minutes and transfer it to a cute sake vessel that can be poured at the table throughout the evening. A rule of thumb for sake is that it's bad luck to pour your own glass, so always pour for others and make sure others always pour for you. Again, I prefer the standard Sho Chiku Bai brand because it's pretty affordable and straightforward in taste.

Hong Kong Cocktail

Makes 1 cocktail

On my last trip to Hong Kong, I stumbled upon a small bar in Kowloon that was serving a drink I will never forget. It was acidic, milky, and so refreshing. I've tried re-creating it ever since and this is as close as I can get. My version uses soda water, which adds a little bubbly to it. For those who don't want the booze, just omit the alcohol from the recipe and it's still a very enjoyable cocktail.

2 strawberry slices

1 sprig fresh mint

1 shot vodka or gin

One 2.1-ounce bottle Yakult or other probiotic milk beverage, such as Calpico

3 ounces sparkling water

Ice

In a cocktail glass, muddle the strawberries and mint together. Add the vodka, Yakult, and sparkling water. Add enough ice to fill the glass. Stir and serve.

The Sake Bomb Game

Serves 6 players

6 glasses of beer

6 sets of chopsticks

6 shot glasses of sake

1 cooked chicken foot

1. Over a cup full of beer, arrange the chopsticks parallel so that the shot glass of sake can rest on them above the beer. Once everyone has their sake/beer arrangement in front of them, you're ready to begin.

2. Count to three and then bang both hands on the table on either side of your glass. Your goal is to get the sake glass to drop down into the beer and then chug it before anyone else. Whoever finishes last has the punishment (or reward, if you ask Mama Fong) of eating a cooked chicken foot.

6 DAYS OUT

Confirm that your guests can make it . . . you don't want an empty seat at hot pot.

3 DAYS OUT

Gather all the equipment and purchase what you don't have: butane burners, back-up butane (very important), wire mesh baskets, and whatever else.

2 DAYS OUT

Do all the shopping for your ingredients. This gives you an extra day just in case you need to go to a different grocery store to pick up the missing pieces.

Buy flowers for the table.

1 DAY OUT

Prep all sturdy ingredients that are able to hold in the fridge overnight (space permitting): napa cabbage, lotus root, meatballs, and fish balls.

Prep the Smashed Radish Salad and let it marinate overnight.

 ## DINNER PARTY!

Clean the house!

Arrange the flowers.

Prep all remaining ingredients: enoki mushrooms, sliced salmon, cubed tofu, chrysanthemum leaves, dandelion leaves.

Plate all prepped ingredients.

Portion the sauces into bowls for the sauce buffet.

Set the table and set up the sauce buffet and drink station.

Start the music!

Acknowledgments

A full-bellied thanks to . . .

Each of our twelve contributors for being the kinds of cooks, hosts, and people who inspire us to cook and gather at home. In an age of increasing isolation, it's hard to think of an act more generous or more human than opening your home and sharing your food. Thank you for the candidness, creativity, and logistical masterminding required to design such beautiful and sharable dinner parties. Thank you to our literary agent, Abigail Walters, for seeing our vision and championing this project from the very beginning. You saw all its potential and more, and we couldn't have done it without you. Special thanks to Fatima Khawaja for helping develop the recipes, and for lending personal, professional, and (also) delicious touches. Thank you to Sarah Kwak, our brilliant editor, for believing in the project and making everything possible. And thank you to Jacqueline Quirk, Bonni Leon-Berman, Rachel Meyers, Chris Andrus, and the rest of the team at Harvest for all the hard work that goes into making a book real.

Thank you to our photographers, Michael Graydon and Nikole Herriot, for joining this project with a vision and seeing it through twelve different shoots in three cities with countless people. We continue to be inspired by their thoughtfulness, creativity, and kindness. Thank you to our longtime contributors Tyna Hoang, for styling the most beautiful foods (and saving bites for everyone on set), and Sam Margherita, for prop styling each shot and tablescape to perfection. Thanks to the many, many other humans who helped make these photoshoots happen from the contributors' friends to those who fed us on those long days.

Thank you to Kim Uong for planting the seed that became this book and for curating the contributors with her good taste (literally). Thank you to Cristala Andrews for her ceaselessly creative art direction, her cleverness, her collaboration, and her vision. Thank you to the executive producer Jamie Arendt for making magic happen, always. And to Shadaylah Byrd for keeping us sane with her organization, forward thinking, and kindness. Thank you to Chef Ed Kernan (and his family!) for testing every single recipe in this cookbook, even when he almost flambéed his eyebrows off. Thanks to Jen Miller for her involvement in all things set and artworks. Thanks to Erika Jaquez and Prae Weissman for beautiful illustrations and delightful designs. Special thanks to Caroline Zavakos for meticulously reading and thinking over every syllable in this book, shaping its narrative, writing odds and ends, and overseeing its creation from start to finish.

Lastly, thank you to my cofounders, Amir & Zach, and every person at Our Place for building a brand rooted in representation that is invested in telling the stories of who we are across the kitchen table. Building this brand together has been the greatest privilege of my life. Together we've created a place where all our traditions are celebrated loudly and proudly. We're all here today cooking and eating and throwing dinner parties together because of what we've built together.

Universal Conversion Chart

Oven temperature equivalents

250°F = 120°C

275°F = 135°C

300°F = 150°C

325°F = 160°C

350°F = 180°C

375°F = 190°C

400°F = 200°C

425°F = 220°C

450°F = 230°C

475°F = 240°C

500°F = 260°C

Measurement equivalents

Measurements should always be level unless directed otherwise.

⅛ teaspoon = 0.5 mL

¼ teaspoon = 1 mL

½ teaspoon = 2 mL

1 teaspoon = 5 mL

1 tablespoon = 3 teaspoons = ½ fluid ounce = 15 mL

2 tablespoons = ⅛ cup = 1 fluid ounce = 30 mL

4 tablespoons = ¼ cup = 2 fluid ounces = 60 mL

5⅓ tablespoons = ⅓ cup = 3 fluid ounces = 80 mL

8 tablespoons = ½ cup = 4 fluid ounces = 120 mL

10⅔ tablespoons = ⅔ cup = 5 fluid ounces = 160 mL

12 tablespoons = ¾ cup = 6 fluid ounces = 180 mL

16 tablespoons = 1 cup = 8 fluid ounces = 240 mL

Index

Note: Page references in italics *indicate photographs.*

HarperCollins books may be purchased for educational, business, or sales promotional use. For information, please email the Special Markets Department at SPsales@ harpercollins.com.

FIRST EDITION

Designed by Bonni Leon-Berman

Photography by Michael Graydon and Nikole Herriott

Food styling by Tyna Hoang

Prop styling by Samantha Margherita

Narrative direction by Caroline Zavakos

The material on linked sites referenced in this book is the author's own. HarperCollins disclaims all liability that may result from the use of the material contained at those sites. All such material is supplemental and not part of the book. The author reserves the right to operate or close the website in his/ her sole discretion following December 2024.

Get bonus content and tools for gathering at fromourplace.com/ cookbook

Library of Congress Cataloging-in-Publication Data has been applied for.

ISBN 978-0-06-333015-3

24 25 26 27 28 IMG 10 9 8 7 6 5 4 3 2 1